The
Black
Student's
Guide
To
Success

www.blackstudentsguide.com

Roderick Claybrooks, M.D.

Published by Plasmid Publishing House, L.L.C

Published by Plasmid Publishing House, L.L.C

visit us online at www.blackstudentsguide.com

Printed in the United States of America

First Printing April 2003

ISBN: 0-615-12376-7

ATTENTION : SCHOOLS AND BUSINESSES

This book is available at quantity discounts with bulk purchase for educational, business, or sales promotional use. For information, please write to: Special Sales Department, Plasmid Publishing House, P.O. Box 39201, Redford, MI. 48239

Mays Printing Company - Detroit - (313) 861-1900
"A Certified Minority Printer"

Contents

INTRODUCTION

In today's world being uninformed can be very costly. You cannot afford to be without proper information. Knowledge is imperative for your survival. I am emphasizing increasing your knowledge and pressing forward in your educational pursuits after seeing first-hand throughout my life what can be the end result when you do not possess it. I believe that placing a lot of focus on education can have a direct positive effect on the quality of your life and the life of your family. I use the word education many times throughout this book, but I do not use it to exclusively mean formal university education in every instance. My hope is that you will increase your knowledge in any avenue available to you. This may mean night classes after you get off from work, or visiting your local bookstore and picking up books on the subjects that interest you. It may mean being personally mentored by someone that is willing to teach you. Whatever source is available to you, please use it to its fullest.

Just living and getting up in the morning to collect a paycheck is not enough if you really want to live the life that you have always wanted to live. The thing that amazes me is that many of us know in our hearts that we are not living out our dreams, and we know that our jobs are not going to take us there, but we continue on the same path anyway. It is time to make an active effort to change our situation. You cannot expect anyone to act on your behalf. You cannot expect anyone to change your life for you.

What do you want out of life? If you ask ten different people, you will likely get ten different answers. There is nothing wrong with that, because we are all looking for something different. The first step in obtaining a lot of things that you want out of life is increasing your knowledge. Do you want a better career than you currently have? This may come after an increase in knowledge. Do you want to make more money? Many times this will require that you increase your knowledge in certain areas. Do you want to stop your sink from leaking? You are going to have to pay someone to fix it or you are going to have to obtain knowledge in that area if you do not already possess it.

We have all heard the statements, 'KNOWLEDGE IS THE KEY or KNOWLEDGE IS POWER'. Many times in the black community we complain about our circumstances. Knowledge and education can change many of these circumstances.

We are living in tremendous times in American history. Information and technology has us moving at such rapid rates. I believe that we are living in a very special time especially for black Americans. I believe that we are afforded opportunities today like no other time in recent history. My grandfather was not in a position to experience what I am currently experiencing. The opportunity to become a surgeon was not available to him. Today a young black person from the projects can one day become a multimillionaire. This country is like no other place on the planet, where an idea alone can become a nationwide movement. Just a thought alone can make you rich. Time after time we hear stories of real life

Cinderella's that were downtrodden in their youth and later grew to become something great.

I believe that we must take advantage of these amazing opportunities available to us. My hope is that our youth use education as the number one weapon in their attempt to achieve success. With knowledge and education many barriers can be broken. With knowledge and education a life in the projects can be left behind. With knowledge and education financial struggles can be eliminated. Knowledge and education can provide you with a different and more fulfilling life.

Today, like never before, we see so many black success stories. We see black judges and lawyers. We see black CEO's of successful companies. In the music industry we have young blacks that control millions of dollars through their corporations. These examples are encouraging but still too few of us are enjoying this success in our own households. To many of us it is just a pleasant story, but not something that we are living ourselves. Too many of us are being left out of the richness that this world has to offer simply because we have not used one of the greatest weapons that God has given us, our brain.

Our brain is one of our greatest assets. By strengthening our brains we can overcome many of the uneven scenarios that we may have been born into. We may not have been born in a nice neighborhood, but a good education can move us out of these neighborhoods or give us the tools to help change these neighborhoods. We may be making minimum wage now, but an education can provide a significant increase in our income. Our families may not have any money to leave to us as an inheritance, but we can change that situation for our children.

Education can literally change your world. It can make a new world for you. As blacks we are very quick to complain about our circumstances, but in my experience, many of us are very slow to make changes to our circumstances. If there is a segment of life that you feel that you are missing out on then you need to increase your knowledge in that area.

You do not have to live a defeated life. The necessary tools for success are within you, but the problem is that they must be cultivated and nurtured. Your talents must be brought out of you. The keys to your success are not going to come from the television or be found at the ballgame. Neither of these things are evil, but if you are so unhappy with your lot in life then why aren't more of your efforts aimed in areas that can change this?

Education and knowledge can take you to a life that your parents and grandparents were never able to enjoy. It can put you in a position to be of assistance to others. It can put you in a position to leave a legacy for your children. It will allow you to be an example to the confused ones among us.

Many of our youth do not see a future for themselves. They don't see a future that is any better than their current circumstances. Many of us have futures that are determined by our physical limitations. When the physical takes us as far as we can go, we give up, and it is the end of the road for us. The day that we realize that we really can't sing very well, our future is over. The day that we realize that we really aren't the athlete that we thought we were, our future is over. If our physical prowess can't get us there then we aren't allowed to go. If I continue to believe that the **only** reason why we are not getting ahead is because we are black, then we will never make it. We have a major say as to what is in our future.

Our potential and our future is limitless. How can we be limitless if we are physically limited? It is because our mental abilities are limitless. One of our greatest assets that God has given us goes untapped, and that is our minds. Knowledge and education opens doors to a different world than we are currently experiencing. When I speak of education, I do not just mean university education. I believe that university education is very important, but the most successful people are not always the people with the most degrees. Bill Gates is one of the richest men in the world, and he did not finish college.

I wrote this book because I have come across too many of our black youth that have not tapped into the almost limitless potential that God has invested in them. Over the past few years I have seen so much wasted talent come through the emergency rooms of

Detroit Hospitals that it is staggering. Our children are no less gifted and no less talented than any other children. Since this is the case, then why aren't more of them going on to greatness? Why are the jails bursting open with black men?

Our children do not want any less out of life than other children. They, like everyone else want to live in a nice home, drive a nice automobile, and have money to spend. This is part of the American dream.

Many of our young men believe that the only way that they will obtain success is on a sports field. Some of our young ladies believe that the only way that they will obtain it is to marry a successful man. This does not have to be the case. One of our greatest assets is sitting right between our ears and it goes underutilized.

It saddens my heart when I ask a fifteen year old kid from Detroit about his plans after high school and he gives me a blank stare like he doesn't have a clue as to what I am talking about. Many of our youth have no plans, they are just living life and will take things as they come. They give me this blank stare because they never have even considered college as an option. They don't even believe that it is there to benefit them. I know exactly how they feel because until I was eighteen years old, I never thought that college was a possibility for me either. I never planned on going because no one told me that it was an option for me. No one explained to me how obtaining an education could expose me to a better life than I had grown accustomed to seeing in my old neighborhood. Because I never saw anyone in that position, it was difficult for me to see myself in that kind of position.

In my neighborhood we didn't have discussions about increasing our knowledge and obtaining financial independence. The only people that appeared to be somewhat independent and financially well-off were the drug dealers.

Education can get you many of the things that you desire out of life. I believe that you have a better chance of getting it through education than any other method. There isn't anything wrong with sports. If you have that level of skill, maximize it to your fullest potential. I wish that I was that gifted. For the rest of us who do not have that option, we are left to use whatever else God has given us to make a living.

For some reason, many of our youth overlook education as a way out of the ghetto. This is a sad mistake that ends up costing them over and over again. Education is one of the surest tickets out of the ghetto. It is much safer than selling drugs, I can promise you that. Since most of us cannot dunk a basketball, we should stick to education as our ticket out.

Our children have become fascinated with what is shown on the television regarding the fairytale lives of the athletes/entertainers. They show their homes, and their enormous salaries, and the fantastic plays that they make. What the television does not tell these children is that they have a better chance of becoming a surgeon than becoming Shaquille O'Neal. Only about 400 men play in the NBA each season. There are hundreds of thousands of doctors in the United States.

They don't tell these children how much being born with a particular body plays into becoming a professional athlete. I am five feet ten inches tall. No matter how often I practice basketball, I will never be six and a half to seven feet tall, which is the height of many NBA players. I was not born with a lot of speed, and it is not difficult to outrun me. But if I study hard, I can change my circumstances. Using our minds makes the playing field more equal, and it overcomes our inability to dunk a basketball.

Where we start off in life is not where we must end up. Use the tools available to you and maximize them to your potential. The following chapters are simple and straightforward. Keep an open mind and read them very carefully.

I have used the word student in the title of the book to emphasize the point that we should be in a learning mode at all times. Do not assume that student is only for kids. This book is for anyone that wants more out of life. Successful people are lifelong learners. They never stop being students.

CHAPTER 1

THE IMPORTANCE OF KNOWLEDGE

"My people are destroyed for the lack of knowledge"
-the prophet Hosea

      I experienced a disturbing situation when my wife and I were trying to purchase our first home. My sister-in-law had informed us of a house that she once visited. She told us about it just in-case the situation did not work out for her and her husband. She described what sounded like a beautiful place to live. As she continued to talk about the home, she pointed out that it had a library in it. At that very moment my wife's younger cousin burst into a chuckle and said, "Library? What do you need a library for?" I did not say anything on the outside, but it bothered me that he found that to be so amusing. He thought that it was some kind of joke. Surely to use a room and fill it with knowledge has got to be a waste. Right? It bothers me that this is the mentality of some of our youth. I have come across too many of our youth that feel that reading and learning is for sissies or nerds and that it is not cool. This is how we have been fooled. This type of thinking is the reason why we need to re-educate some of our youth and re-program them. This type of thinking is what causes us to be left behind the rest of society, and causes us to crowd the welfare offices of America, begging for handouts. It leads to a life of unfulfilled dreams, and causes second, third, and fourth generations to be born, live, and die in the housing projects of the urban slums.

Some of us have allowed outside forces to dictate to our children what is and what is not important. Unfortunately, some of our children believe that education is not important. By the time many of them find out just how important it is they have gotten themselves into situations that make it difficult for them to go back to school.

Some of us played games throughout our youth, and during situations when we should have been learning. Once we decide to get our acts together it becomes very difficult and frustrating when we attempt to absorb new concepts and information because we have never taken the time to develop any study habits. When we do make an attempt to go back, we get so frustrated because the material seems so difficult and we want to give up. For many of us this is the end of the road and we settle for some low paying job.

Others, instead of focusing on education, have engaged in physical relationships that have produced children. They feel that now they can't go back because of work obligations that they must honor to feed the family. Others have accumulated so much debt that decreasing their work hours to attend classes seems virtually impossible because all of the bills that they have to pay.

Since I am not that old, I can distinctly remember how un-cool it was to even appear to be smart. If you received a grade higher than a C+, people were looking at you like you were an alien, and were ready to call the government to have you taken away. You would immediately be dismissed as a nerd and teased, taunted, and placed into exile for getting good grades. All the while not realizing how foolish we really were.

If we are really honest with ourselves, the concept of being smart as the wrong thing to do is actually one of the dumbest routes in life to take. Why would you not want to be smart? Who was the idiot who said that there is glory in being dumb? What is so cool about being dumb? What can you accomplish by being dumb? How much money can you make when you are dumb? Who can you help when you are dumb? Think about it and decide what road in life you want to take.

Some of our children do not believe that education will have any kind of positive impact on their lives. They have been tricked into believing that education will not help them achieve their dreams. Because of this they seek other alternatives to achieve their goals in life. All too often they give up on life and themselves too young, and accept an alternative method to get what they want.

For a while I started to think that some of our children do not do as well as they should in the educational arena because they do not believe in themselves. I no longer believe that this is the case. I have found that when a young person actually believes in something, they go at it full steam ahead and give it 100 percent. I noticed that when they take the alternate route, it is done with just as much enthusiasm or effort. Since they really believe in this alternate road, they work very hard at it. This being the case, they need to believe and understand that education and knowledge can change their lives for the better. Maybe if they start to believe in education then they will stick with it.

I grew up in Detroit and have known many young men that have chosen to live the life of crime and sell drugs. They put their heart and soul into what is known as the 'Drug Game'. They master the distribution of their product and know their system and their market as well as any Harvard finance graduate knows the NYSE or the NASDAC. Many of these men on the higher levels of the drug game run their operation with the efficiency and structure of any large corporation. They have certain workers that perform certain roles within the organization. They have workers that do pickups and drop-offs. Some workers are responsible for mixing and packaging the drugs, while others are responsible for running and managing certain drug houses that the organization owns.

I do not believe that they would participate in such risky behavior if they did not believe that their participation would be in their benefit in the long run. You can contrast this with the possibility that they see no other alternative to improve their situation. Regardless of their reasoning it becomes an obvious waste of intelligence and talent. Regardless of the bias we have about the morality of the activity, it takes intelligence and leadership ability to run a successful major drug operation. The government had to get Al Capone on tax charges because he was too smart for them to catch him doing other illegal activities. The management of multiple levels of workers along with the production and distribution of products to various locations are skills that corporate America uses everyday and is greatly rewarded.

The problem is that the use of these skills in literally a dead end job like selling drugs is an example of wasted talent. I believe that if many of our dead or imprisoned young black men could have been caught and taught early on the benefit of knowledge, then we could have hundreds or maybe thousands of legal multimillionaires.

I can remember once watching a documentary on a cable channel one Saturday afternoon. The focus of the documentary was death row inmates. They were interviewing an inmate that had been scheduled to die very soon who had been incarcerated for over twenty years. This documentary was a very revealing experience. Many of these hardened criminals admitted that this is not a place where you want to end up. They tried to express how they made wrong decisions and became involved in the wrong things with the wrong crowd. As a result they were living a wasted life, and would never experience the joys that this life has to offer.

Of the many inmate interviews I watched, one man has remained on my mind many years later. As I already stated, this man was scheduled to die soon. He had been convicted for killing another man. I will never forget the last part of that interview. His statement was as follows:

> "I don't regret the fact that I will die soon. I killed another man, and I deserve to die for that. The thing that I regret the most is that now I really understand that I could have been anything that I wanted to be. Here I have been sitting in these jail cells for all of these years and now I truly know in my heart that I could have been any thing that I could have put my mind to. Now it is too late."

Unfortunately this is when many of our young people find out that they really could have been somebody, way too late. If we can get people to understand the importance of knowledge early in their lives, then we will hear fewer and fewer stories like this.

We must come to understand the importance of knowledge, and the difference that it can make in our lives. We must not just obtain knowledge, but we must also focus on the application of knowledge. Knowledge can no longer be something that we stumble upon. It must become something that we diligently seek if we are to ever change our circumstances.

It will do you no good to accumulate knowledge if you are not going to apply it to your life. Knowing that a red light means stop doesn't do you any good if you continue to drive right through the intersection. Most of us know a 'Barber Shop Scholar'-- some self proclaimed 'know it all' in all areas. They know this and they know that but they actually produce very little.

Knowledge is critical to your survival in this harsh world, since ignorance is so dangerous today. I know that there are many places in life that you want to go, and I promise you that knowledge can get you there once it starts to become a large part of your life.

We must get our children to understand the importance of education. They need to understand the importance of all forms of education, not just university education. They must understand that education is vital, not optional. Reading should not just be something that you do when you are bored, it should be the primary thing that you do. Then if you have extra time, go to the television, but not the television first. THE TELEVISION PROVIDES YOU WITH VERY LITTLE TO BETTER YOUR CIRCUMSTANCES. If you want out of the projects the solution won't come from the television. If you want a better life it will not come through the television.

Knowledge is power. The problem is that everyone wants power but very few want to do what it takes to obtain it. We want the praise and benefits that come with power, but we don't want to work for it. Knowledge does not just fall from the sky. We must seek it diligently. I believe that once our children are taught the importance of knowledge, then the problems that ignorance creates will diminish.

We go after things that are important to us with purpose and passion. You go to the grocery store to obtain food because you know that you will perish without it. You go to the grocery store when it is raining, snowing, or whatever. Nothing is going to stop you from getting to the grocery store. You have full understanding that you cannot live without that food. Once we come to the understanding that the lack of knowledge is one of the key reasons for our destruction today we will also realize that we cannot truly live without it.

CHAPTER 2

ACTING WHITE

"Death and Life are in the Power of the Tongue"
-King Soloman

I know someone out there is asking, "What is this all about?" I know that the term sounds absolutely ridiculous, and you are right because it is just that. It is ridiculous that we even have to take time to discuss such an issue. In the times that we live in we should have progressed well beyond things like this, but unfortunately we haven't. I should modify this by saying that some of us have not progressed beyond this. It is things like this and the mentality that propels such a statement from some people's mouths that are some of the very shackles that keep us chained to the welfare line. I believe that today one of our greatest fights is against our own destructive mentality. I believe that if we can elevate our mind, then we can elevate a nation.

So for those of you that really don't know what this means, good for you. Just move on to the next chapter because if you haven't been stained with hearing this foolishness then there is no need to start now. I would hate to be the one that even sparked this conversation at your lunch table tomorrow. For the rest of us, let's address this quickly and move on.

The term 'acting white' is used in many of our predominantly black schools and neighborhoods. It is a label that is given to some of our black youth, and even adults, that engage in situations that are considered 'white' people activities. Some of these include: attempting to achieve highly at academics, speaking proper American English as taught in our current school system; as an adult, moving from the 'hood' to a predominantly white neighborhood. There are probably many other situations in which this occurs, but these are the ones that really stick out in my mind.

I have personally seen people ridiculed when being involved in these types of situations. Many times when I was younger, even when I was not getting the best grades in the world, I saw those that actually deserved praise for their efforts being shot down by their peers for their accomplishments. If they were accepted into honors societies or getting too many of the answers correct, then they were told that they were trying to be 'white'. What is so crazy about this is that the people who have this type of mentality are really perpetuating a self defeating attitude about themselves and others like them. Telling a child that they are acting other than themselves when they achieve something great is like telling that child that nothing is expected of them. It is like achieving greatness is totally out of character for them. This just shows that the person making such a statement also expects nothing of themselves or their race and does not have a clue about their true heritage.

A child that is getting good grades and being accepted into honors societies should be encouraged and assisted to flourish. Instead, people who don't understand very much crush these children's egos. When you tell an academic all-star that they are acting white by doing well in school, you are stating that white is equated with success so naturally black is equated with failure.

Peer pressure is very strong, and the need to fit in affects children differently. This type of isolation has affected some of our brightest stars in ways that we can never imagine. Social interaction is very important to all of us, even the strongest among you. Who knows how many Ben Carsons we have assassinated with our poison arrows of ignorance?

This concept is very difficult for me to grasp. The whole idea is completely baffling to me, I just do not get it. It is absolutely amazing that some of our people have been convinced that high achievement or even the attempt at improving their situation is a bad thing. Especially considering how many Black Americans come from some of the worst scenarios that this country has to offer. Many of us have been born and raised in the financial and social despair of the urban ghettos.

This reminds me of some of the stories that we have been taught about slavery. We have come to learn that some slaves thought that it was foolish to make an attempt at freedom. It is safe to say that brave souls like Harriet Tubman felt that by staying in her current situation, she was already dead. I felt the same way about my old neighborhood. Although I didn't have a specific plan when I left for college, it was obvious to me that my life was not going to get any better just sitting around on the porch and drinking beer all day. In my mind I had absolutely nothing to lose by leaving. At the very worst I would come back home to the 'hood' where I was loved and accepted.

As many slaves in the past were convinced that attempting to leave was foolish and useless, many of our youth today feel similar pressure when they are ridiculed for wanting to move on to better things. Just sit and ponder this scenario for a moment. Think about how mentally crushed some of our people had to be during those times. A person's mind has to be a long way gone to believe that working from sun up to sun down, sleeping in a barn, exposed to be beaten or killed at will is better than running away.

As hard as this is to understand, it still occurs on a smaller scale today. Many second and third generation slaves could not see freedom as a possibility. Any talk of taking a stab at freedom, or a better life up North or in Canada, was crazy talk to them. Today we raise second, third, and fourth generations in the projects. Many of these people do not see the possibility of a better life through academics as a reality. In their mind if you're trying to do anything other than what your mother, your father, or your grandparents did, you are crazy. The belief that things are just fine the way that they are is so strong that they exile and isolate those who think different. Unfortunately this peer pressure causes some of our youth to fold. I have seen those that have been completely isolated at some point in their life due to their achievements attempt to feed their hunger for acceptance to the point of destroying their own future.

I know a young man that graduated from high-school with a 3.76 GPA. He was what people would call a 'nerd'. He was a very nice, intelligent guy, but he was not one of the 'fellas', so to speak. He had never been a part of the 'in crowd'. He even went to the prom by himself because he didn't have a date.

Are you starting to see the flaws in this mentality? Here we have a young man that doesn't address our young women by calling them 'female dogs' and 'garden tools'. You know what I mean. He doesn't sell or use drugs. He has been accepted into a Big Ten university on a partial scholarship, and has all the potential that you can ask for in a young man. Instead of girls fighting to get next to him, he has absolutely no date at all. He came to the prom all by himself. Unfortunately some of our young ladies are attracted to young men with not even one-half the potential that he had. Some of our young ladies attach themselves to young men that are not going to help them reach their own potential.

Be honest with me. Tell me what you would think of me if I willingly engaged in the following scenario. Assume that I wanted to go to Chicago. Even though this is where I desire to end up, I accept and pay for an airplane ticket that takes me and leaves me in Texas. You would tell me that I was stupid probably. Before you tell me this you would probably ask me why I would do such a thing.

Why on earth would you accept a ride that is taking you the opposite from where you want to be?

It does seem foolish, but many times our young people attach themselves to people that are going in the exact opposite direction that they want to go in. At the same time the pilots that are going towards our desired destination (success) are shot down in mid-flight by character assassination with the use of words.

Let's get back to the young man that I knew in high-school. When he arrived at college he changed into a different person. In a completely new environment, around an entirely new group of people who didn't know him or his past, he had an opportunity for a rebirth. He was able to fashion a new character for himself. None of these new kids knew about his past pressures. They didn't know that he was pressured into doing work for the more popular guys back in high school, or that he was poked and prodded for answers on homework assignments and tests by these same guys. They had no idea that he would write the program in computer class and everyone else would just copy it from him. Many times he gave in to such pressure thinking that if he gave in and helped one of these guys, eventually they will see him as one of them, right? Wrong. When we give in to such pressures, most often it only labels us as weak and willing to go along with whatever. Your improved position and status is only short lived until your usefulness has run out.

None of the girls on the college campus knew that he went to the prom without a date. Because he left his old environment he did actually recreate himself. The results, I am sure, are not what he had expected.

He hung out with the popular crowd, went to all the parties, and did all the things that all guys did. He wore the latest fashions and spoke the lingo. He had the latest music and was now a drinker, to put it lightly. Honestly, by the end of the third semester you did not want to challenge him to a drinking contest. He nick-named himself 'Leadbelly' because he could drink volumes of alcohol that would make other guys sick. He participated in all the pranks and gags that college kids get involved in. The problem was that this was a shock to his system and he couldn't handle it. When you take a fresh water fish and throw it into salt water it is going to have a very difficult time surviving. Even though both environments are water the conditions are very different.

He left high school with a 3.76 grade point average and a partial scholarship to a Big Ten university. After the first semester in college he was on academic probation. After the third semester he was out of school with a final GPA of 0.082. The last time I heard anything about him he was working midnights in a mailroom somewhere with a baby on the way.

Do not let others perception of you and your goals steer you from your path of success. If they think that aiming high is a bad thing, then so be it. Life has a way of playing cruel tricks on us. Some of those that taunt and tease and accuse our young stars of 'Acting White' will be asking for your business card ten years later. They will be asking if you could 'hook them up' with a job. Some of these young ladies ten years later will be on their fourth child by the fourth father, all the while wondering what could have been. Stay strong and stay focused.

CHAPTER 3

Success is Not an Accident

I would like you to think for a moment about some of the people that you admire. Get a good mental picture in your head about some people that you consider to be highly successful in their field of choice. In sports we think of people like Michael Jordan and Muhammad Ali. In business we think of people like Bill Gates and Jack Welch. The list goes on and on of successful people that are around us. These people have surpassed what the majority of society has achieved in their respective fields.

Today with the availability of media resources, we have lots of access to small facets of these people's lives. Many times biographies and television shows chronicle these people's lives and even show their homes. We see the kinds of cars they drive and acreage that surrounds their home.

What many of us forget is that we are seeing these people at one short period of time in their lives. It is literally like a snap shot in a photo album. Many of these depictions appear to be very intimate and revealing and at times can give us the false sense that we really know these people. Seeing people for very short bursts of time never really gives you an appreciation for what they have been through and what it took for them to get to where they stand now.

The snapshots don't show how much effort and time it really took to achieve such high levels of success. We see Tiger Woods hit a ball with great accuracy, precision, and power. What we don't see is how many practice hours it took for him to be able to do what he does. We don't know how many parties and ball games he had to forgo with his friends because he had to practice. All we see is the result.

What is the result? The result is that he has achieved financial security, and if he so chooses, his finance and influence can make changes in many people's lives. He has achieved the highest level of success in his field.

Because of his preparation, he is no longer the borrower, but he can now become the lender. When he goes to the car dealer he isn't begging for a lower interest rate. They are rolling out the red carpet and getting him whatever he wants. And don't sit there and say that this could never be you. Get that defeated mentality out of your mind. Start to expect greatness for yourself.

His dedication to his goal and his level of success has given him more control over his life than most of us will ever enjoy. Many of us have the false sense of security that a job title, salary, and benefits gives us. This makes many of us feel that we are very much in control. Many of us have not come to the understanding that without independence and financial security, at any given moment our small world can come crumbling down.

You give the best years of your life and the prime period of your health to a company, yet you can't even afford to take a leave of absence for a significant period of time. That's not being in control, that is servitude. Then we retire when we are old but soon after that the health problems start, and we are unable to fully enjoy the golden years of our lives.

People do not make it to financial freedom and independence by the luck of the draw. I do not believe in luck. If you plant apple seeds, an apple tree will grow. We get to high levels of success by calculated actions and dedication to a formulated plan.

Other people's success and achievements sound good and look good, but when we find out what the requirements are to get to the same level we often times give up and shy away.

During my freshman year in college many people were pre-med or pre-law students. As the years went on, many of these students dropped off one by one. The glamour and appeal of something often greatly overshadows the hard work it takes to achieve that goal.

Wealth is not accidental. If you think your financial security will come from a lottery ticket, then write me and I'll send you one of mine. I'll make one up just for you.

Wealth is not accidental nor is success. In fact, it is quite the opposite. It is calculated and planned. Tiger does not hit the ball the way that he does because he showed up on a golf course when he was eighteen years old and decided to start playing. That was just the age that many of us saw him for the first time. He planned to hit that ball the way he does before we even knew who he was.

I do hundreds of operations a year. The fact that I can perform certain operations is not because of what I have done the day that I meet the patient, but what I did years before I ever met the patient. Before the patient ever knew who I was I planted seeds in this area. The skills I obtained to perform operations were intentionally achieved, not just stumbled upon. It took me countless hours of study to be able help people in this capacity.

Many of us are filled with dreams and desires. Many of us have tons of goals that we would like to achieve. Few of us have a specific plan written down, step by step on how to achieve it. I did not say in your head, but written down on paper to see and review and adjust as needed. Just like mowing the lawn and doing laundry, many things that we put in our mental to-do box get shoved aside until there is a time that is more convenient for us.

You cannot approach your success as a convenience but you must approach it as a requirement. In fact, I suggest to you that if your preparation is great enough, your success will become second nature instead of a hopeful accomplishment.

I think that one of our major problems is that we confuse what we want with what we expect. We quickly tell people how we want to be financially secure. We tell people how we want to go back to school. We tell people that we want to own our own business. However, many times wants and desires do not equate with expectations. Do you really expect to be successful or do you just want to be successful?

For some of us our self image is so low that we don't expect better for ourselves. Many of us do not expect more for our race as a whole. We must escape this self destructive thinking. People around you that do not believe in the success and potential of our people can poison your dreams. That is why your environment is so important.

When we get a good idea or opportunity what is one of the first things that we go and do? We go and tell someone. Unfortunately many times we go and tell someone that is doing absolutely nothing positive in their own lives. We confide in people that have produced absolutely nothing at all. So what is their response to our hopes and dreams? "You must be crazy, that will never work." Then that idea that you thought was so great suddenly does not sound so great anymore. It is not that the greatness left, but now your expectation is no longer there.

A farmer with bare crops is not the farmer that you want to be giving you advice on how to plant your crops. You want to share your dreams with a successful farmer.

So why do I say that there is a difference between wanting something and expecting something? Many of us want to be successful, but how many of us really expect to be successful? As you build your confidence and self worth so will your expectations rise.

One of the major differences between wanting and expecting

16

is your approach to them. When you *want* something, there can be a tendency to be complacent and allow things to happen and come to you. When you *expect* things to happen, many times your participation is one of action with regard to the situation in question. You don't just let the chips fall where they may, you play an active role in where the outcome lies.

I am awful when is comes to landscaping and gardening and maintaining a beautiful looking lawn. Even when I could have used the money for something else, I paid a man to cut our lawn every week.

When we moved into the house there was a bed of flowers in the front yard. Neither my wife nor I maintained it, so it became overgrown with weeds. I removed the wooden boarder that surrounded the plants and moved the dirt. No grass grew in that spot. I wanted grass to grow in the spot where the plants used to be but it didn't. My only active role in my hope that grass would grow was to remove the old weeds and dig up that old dirt. I really *wanted* grass to grow, but for a whole summer I had a big triangle shape of dirt on my front lawn where I *wanted* grass to grow.

Now let's add to the situation. Let's say that now I go out and turn over the soil properly, plant some grass seed, add some fertilizer, and then start to water the grass on a regular basis. Because of the actions on my part, I no longer just *want* the grass to grow, now I *expect* grass to grow in that bare area on my lawn. Expectation usually involves an entirely different set of actions in comparison to just wanting something.

Success is not an accident, it occurs through constant active intentional intervention on the part of the individual. You don't accidentally become successful, period.

An *expecting* mother is different from a woman that *wants* to become pregnant. Take time to nurture and then birth your visions and dreams from within you. An *expecting* mother has an entirely different routine than a woman that *wants* to become pregnant.

A woman that *wants* to become pregnant may still smoke and drink. A pregnant woman that is *expecting* is willing to change to bring forth what is inside her. Because her mind set has now shifted from just *wanting* to *expecting*, she understands and makes efforts to avoid things that may cause harm to that which she expects to bring forth.

The routines of an *expecting* woman are different than a woman that *wants* to become pregnant. Most women of child bearing age go to the doctor once a year unless other problems arise. An *expecting* woman has many more doctor appointments over the same ten-month time frame. Why? Because the doctor wants to chart the progress and make sure that everything is going as *expected*. People that just *want* to be successful often sit and daydream of what it would be like. Successful people constantly chart their progress in relation to where they *expect* to be. What's my net worth? Am I on course to retire when I want to? What is my market share? What was last years return on my investments? What is my projected revenue over the next five years?

Over half of your success is in your preparation. We usually prepare for things that we expect to happen. If you are expecting company to come over what do most of us do? We get up and clean up the house. Expectation brings a total different mentality. You should expect greatness. Success is not an accident, it is not some random occurrence that falls from the sky. Do not wait for someone to just come up to you and hand you your dreams on a platter. You're in the buffet line man. You better get up and get you some.

CHAPTER 4

COUNT THE COST

"For which of you, intending to build a tower, sitteth not down first, and counteth the cost, whether he have sufficient to finish it?"

-Jesus the Christ

Nothing in this world is free. Whether or not you want to believe it, everything comes with a price and success is no exception. The problem is that most people are not willing to pay what it costs to become successful. We often give a lot of lip service about how much we want success, but do we really want it? I think that it just sounds good to us to tell people how much we want it. That is why people stay put and complain about their situation. That is why they stay on jobs that they hate, jobs that are paying poor wages and giving little respect. They stay on jobs with no opportunity for advancement in position, power, or salary. They stay because it takes less energy to sit back and complain instead of getting up and doing something about it. It costs less to be a sheep instead of a shepard.

Are you willing to pay the cost of what it will really take for you to reach your dreams? Reaching your goals may cost you lots of money. Reaching your goals may cost you lots of your time. Reaching your goals may also cost you lots of your freedom. It may even cost you your friends and family. You need to answer these questions before you embark on this long journey called success.

Some of you may be saying, "How is this going to cost me so much money?" "Success is supposed to make me money, not cost me money." Financing education is a very difficult thing for many black kids. Many of us don't have families that can readily support tens of thousands of dollars in tuition bills. So when we do make it to school, many of us are paying our bills with loans. This money needs to be paid back to their respective lenders, with interest accrued. The last thing you want to do is rack up big bills from student loans and be unable to pay them back because you dropped out in the middle.

I have known many people that have had their credit ruined and even their wages garnished because of unpaid student loan debt. You don't want to be working a full time job somewhere and get denied a purchase of a car or some other big ticket item because of your credit scores. Imagine working a full work week and when your paycheck comes only receiving part of it because your debts are being subtracted from your gross even before you see it. I have known people that have had their income tax refunds taken from them because of unpaid student loan debt.

This is no small endeavor. You have to be serious when you sign your name on the line to accept those checks, because those lenders are going to be really serious when it is time to collect their funds and believe me, they are not going to forget or lose track of you. It is not worth wrecking your financial future if your heart is not in it in the first place. You would be better off accepting a temporary position somewhere until you get your thoughts and plans together. This way you waste less time and you waste less money.

Both my undergraduate school and medical school tuition and fees were quite reasonable when compared to many other universities and medical schools across the country. My medical school tuition was about ten-thousand dollars per year, which is cheap when it comes to medical school. Even still, after it was all said and done, with interest included, I accumulated over one-hundred thousand dollars of debt from my educational costs when combining undergraduate and medical school. This is even after receiving over thirty-thousand dollars in scholarships and grants over the course of my academic career. So as you can see, you really have to be serious because a one-hundred thousand dollar bill is not to be taken lightly. I was over one-hundred thousand dollars in the hole before I had even purchased a home to have a roof over my head. If my heart had not really been into what I was doing and attempting to accomplish this would be a very depressing scenario. Even more importantly, if I had not put myself in the financial position to pay my loans off, this would have caused even more anxiety for me.

Are you willing to carry such a large or even larger financial burden to reach your dreams of success? Many of you may have dreams of opening your own business someday. This is going to cost money, and a lot of it may be your own out of pocket money. Establishing credit is very difficult for new small businesses and unless you have lots of investors lined up, you may have to be willing to sell things off to get started. Trust me I am speaking from experience. You must be willing to sacrifice some things to get started. This could mean no extra money to spend on weekends while you attempt to save and invest in your business, or no new additions to your wardrobe for many months at a time. Being a surgery resident was very helpful to me in this sense, because I seemed to live in hospital scrubs during my first two years of training. There were times when I didn't buy new clothes for over a year since I wore scrubs to work everyday. You may have to sacrifice buying new CD's or DVD's every week. Whatever your tastes are, you will have to curb your appetite and go on a financial diet to make your future a healthy one.

Quite honestly some of us are not willing to do this, which is fine as long as you are happy with your life. However, it bothers me when I hear people complain about their circumstances but do absolutely nothing to change them. If you are unhappy with your current circumstances but you wake up every single morning and apply the exact same approach then nothing will begin to change for you.

What else may success cost you? One of the biggest prices that I have had to pay is lost time with my family and friends. You can watch as many television programs as you want about medicine, or set your VCR to capture every episode of ER if you like. But you will still never have a full grasp of the toll it actually takes to become a surgeon unless you physically and mentally experience it for yourself. Almost all of my twenties is a blur to me. I really don't have very many memories of them because I am always so busy.

I graduated from high school at eighteen years old. Once I got myself on track and realized that I wanted to become a doctor, I was no longer drinking and going to parties, I was in the library. I was accepted into medical school December 23rd of my senior year in college, and I started classes the following fall. Medical school included four more years of classes, study sessions, and reviews. After completion of medical school I was accepted into an orthopaedic surgery residency training program.

My residency included a full work day followed by reading at night. On my longest rotations, my work day could last anywhere from five in the morning to seven at night. And these were the days when I wasn't on call. When I was on call, my days could stretch through the afternoon or night of the following day.

For most occupations, you can leave your work on your desk when you go home. The education of a surgeon is a life-long quest. You can never know it all because it is simply too much information. So after taking care of patients all day, we should go home and learn everything about the diseases that we are treating. We are also responsible for learning how to perform the necessary surgeries that treat some of these conditions, as well as any medicines that may assist us in treatment. We have to have a grasp of anatomy, biology, and physiology. Some of my work weeks have been over one-hundred hours long inside the hospital. While most people work a forty-hour work-week, I have sometimes worked over forty hours straight, with no sleep, at times having completed this before Tuesday even rolls around.

I went to medical school and trained in my hometown, and there were times when I went weeks without seeing my parents because I was always just so busy. When you have a lot of responsibility you can't just shoot out to the stadium with the boys whenever you get ready or just up and go to the movies with your girlfriend whenever you want to. Success is very jealous too. It will leave if you do not pay it close enough attention.

I have not fallen out with nor do I have any bad feelings about my friends from my old neighborhood or college, but I still don't see them very often. Because I have been so busy over the years our relationships have been relegated to very occasional meetings here and there. This is not by choice by any means, but it seems to have worked out this way. So you have to keep this in mind before embarking on this journey. You must ask yourself if you are willing to pay what it may potentially cost you.

By the same token, there are some friendships that should intentionally be terminated. There are some people that will be a direct hindrance to your success if you allow them to stay around. This is a very heavy price to pay for success. Are you willing to pay it?

I touched briefly on the loss of freedom aspect on the road of success. If you are really serious about your goals, it will cost you a lot of your freedom. Free will and doing what I want is a very popular American concept. When your friends are at the bar, you will need to be in the library. When your friends are at the mall, you will need to be in the library. When your friends are playing video games, you will need to be at the library. Sometimes success can be a cage in and of itself. It will lock you at your desk to do work when you really would rather be doing other things. It must be tended to, and it must be nurtured, or you not only will be unable to obtain it, you will also be unable to maintain it.

So I want you to look inside of yourself and check the balance of your account. Do you have enough in you to pay and sacrifice what it's going to cost to succeed in this world?

Please do not get discouraged by what I have said here. I don't want you going away with the impression that success is a torture chamber that will lock you up and make the remainder of your existence a miserable one. I just don't want you to think that it is a free ride. Many 'master plans' get aborted after people realize just how much work it takes to bring the plan into fruition. I think I knew more pre-med and pre-law students in my first two years of college than any other major. That's because most people don't know what it takes to be accepted into higher levels of graduate education. Many people go down these paths because it sounds good and looks cool on television. You have to always count the costs, because nothing in life is free.

In reality if you really love what you do then the sacrifices will be worth it. Even after all I have been through in my years of training there is no other job that I would prefer besides being a surgeon. If God told me that I could have only one job, and I was allowed to choose what it would be, then this would be it. When I am in the operating room it does not feel like work because I enjoy it so much.

In contrast, I have had many jobs that I found absolutely no enjoyment in. What I have found is that even if the shift is only for a few hours per day, it feels like an eternity. They say that time flies when you are having fun and I agree. I have also learned that the exact opposite can be true. Giving up a little freedom and some of your time may be worth putting yourself and your family into a more enjoyable position. However, getting to this better position will require that you give something up. Liken it to paying a toll to get onto the road to success. The fee at the toll booth is different for different people. What I have had to give up may be different from what you will be required to give up. In a twist on the same scenario, what I am willing to give up is also different than what some people are willing to give up.

On the one hand I am trying to get you to understand that in order to get a lot you have to be willing to give a lot. Also please understand that there is a limit to everything. There should even be a limit to what you are willing to pay for your success. It can take a lifetime to build respect and only a second to lose it. No position, or amount of money, or anything else is worth your integrity and your self-respect. On the road of success you will pass many people and interact with many people that will attempt to get you to compromise your standards. Stand strong because in the end it is not worth it.

Over the years many people have sold themselves for riches and positions. You must remember that in the end you have to live with your decisions. You are the one that has to look at that face in the mirror in the morning. Many people who are honest will admit that they regret compromising their integrity to improve their position in life. They realized later that it really wasn't worth it. This is because your personal value cannot be matched with a price of any magnitude.

Compromising who you are as a person can come in many forms. Many of our women are subjected to sexual advances by men in powerful positions. Although not always direct but sometimes implied, these advances are to be connected with advancement of some form or another. STAY STRONG.

Many people are asked to compromise by participating in illegal activity. If not asked to participate directly, sometimes we are asked to just look the other way. STAY STRONG.

Maintaining your integrity and being an honest person may cause you some flack and some criticism. You can't let that sway you to the other side though. Do not think that if you don't fall in line with everyone else then you will never make it, because this is just not true.

When you finally make it, you want it to be with a clean conscious and a clean slate. You don't want anyone to be able to hold things over your head or have you in their back pocket because of the dirt they have on you.

Success costs but the rewards are as great as the costs. You are giving up some freedoms to obtain other freedoms. It is like an exchange program. The freedom that success brings far out weighs the things you will have to give up to obtain that success.

My advice is that you sit down and count all of the costs before you embark on this journey called success. I want you to ask yourself if you are really willing to pay the cost. If you can answer this question in the beginning then it may save you the heartache later. If you are not willing to pay the cost then there is no shame in it. You will just have to live with that decision and the resulting consequences.

CHAPTER 5

DISPEL THE MYTHS

Throughout my journey it has given me great pleasure to see the shocked looks on people's faces when I tell them that I am a college graduate and that I am from a city like Detroit. Right or wrong, we all have some preconceived notions about someone or something. When we do not have personal experiences with something, we tend to rely on what we have heard from others. If we hear this same viewpoint enough times, then it can start to become real to us. (If we do not have an open mind.) If enough people wear a particular fashion, especially famous people, it usually becomes the 'in thing'. Most of us will consider it attractive, if we are hearing these things from people that we respect or trust. A lot of times, our thoughts and opinions are based solely on what we have been told and not necessarily on what we have experienced.

Stereotypes can work in a similar fashion. We have all heard negative things about other groups or races. These comments are usually stated as if it includes everyone in that particular category, and it gives the perception that everyone in that group is exactly alike. These statements paint a group with a very broad brush. The disturbing thing is that most of us experience this at such a young age, when our attitudes are being shaped for us, instead of us learning and judging from our own experiences. When this happens while we are so vulnerable it tends to stick with some of us for a very long time.

Unfortunately some of us hold on to stereotypes that we heard as youngsters and end up perpetuating the same attitude in our children. Some common stereotypes regarding Black people are that we're lazy, stupid, criminals, ignorant, and inferior. When I was growing up, I heard stereotypes that all white people were racists and that all whites hated all black people. It wasn't until I was in my mid-teens and had worked with different races of people that I found this to be untrue. I learned that we have to judge everyone as individuals and give everyone the benefit of the doubt. I could have very easily held on to all of the lies that the other kids told me, but I allowed my personal experience to mold me instead.

You must remember that even though you will be giving everyone else the benefit of the doubt, not everyone will be returning the favor. Even though we would like to think that we live in a color-blind society, we have to be honest with ourselves and realize that we do not. I never let it bother me in the large lecture halls of Michigan State University when some students would stare at me with amazement as if to say, "What is he doing here?" And bear in mind this is not some prestigious Ivy League school. Some people just have a hard time seeing us in a positive role. On my first day of medical school, I noticed several students who almost got whiplash from turning around so fast when a few friends and I walked into the class.

I am no fool, so I know that there are some people that still think black = inferior. But I have used this to my advantage and promising myself that I would never prove these people right has put a fire in me that I cannot quince. I am always prepared for any assignment or presentation to the best of my ability, and I always try to present myself in a professional manner. I always try to have the right answers and try to get 100% on every exam. Why do I do this? Because looking stupid is no fun and even though we have all been there, I just choose not to return. It is very motivating to me to prove people wrong, even though I never say, "I told you so."

I also do it for another reason, I do it for you. You, meaning any black student that is coming after me, young or old. I know that if I mess up, it makes it harder for anyone following me to get a fair chance. If I mess up, I know that there will be someone in the corner saying, "See I told you so, those blacks just can't cut it, maybe we should cut down on hiring them." On the other hand, I also know that if I do well, it will make it easier for you and be more acceptable to work with and associate with you. If I do well, a young black child will be able to look at me and feel that they can be successful also.

When I was in medical school, I went to Harvard to do a rotation in Pediatric Orthopaedic Surgery at Boston Children's Hospital. I remember having an interesting conversation with one of the nurses whom I had been working with for about three weeks at this particular time. On multiple occasions in the past I had mentioned things to her about my hometown, Detroit. One day she came up to me, started a conversation, and asked me, "So you're from the suburbs surrounding Detroit, you're not from the city itself, right?" I replied, "No I actually am from the city itself and have never lived in the suburbs. Actually my parents still live in the house that I grew up in." She had the most puzzled look on her face. I don't think that she believed anyone who was born and raised in Detroit could present themselves in an intelligent and professional manner, even in the midst of some famous people within the world of medicine. She probably felt this way because Detroit has a very bad reputation world wide. It was once the murder capital of the world. For the most part, only the negative aspects of Detroit are brought up or displayed in the news in other cities across the country. Because of all of the negative publicity, people have preconceived notions about the people of Detroit. I know that I have made some people more open minded about inner cities and showed them that rumors and stereotypes do not include everyone. You should always be aware of this and know that what you do does not only affect you, but can affect other people even if they are not related to you. So because of the myths, many times we are painted as all being alike.

The message that I want you to get is to do your very best at each opportunity, regardless of your endeavors. I cannot stand to even lose at checkers or stupid card games. Doing your best has a lot of benefits. One reason being that it will increase your chances of becoming successful at whatever you are trying to accomplish. Another reason being that it will open other doors for you. I have discovered that if you are good at what you do, it doesn't matter what negative things people have to say about you, or what myths they believe about you. When you know your stuff, you cannot be disputed. No one can question why you were given a particular position or promotion. No one can question why they hired that black person. Your skills and talents will speak for themselves. Again, do your very best at each opportunity and try to learn something every chance you get, and you will be able to dispel the myths.

I really hate to say it. Trust me, I really do not want to tell you this, but I must warn you. A lot of the doubt, put-downs, and disbelief in your possible success will come from your own community. It may even come from your own family. It will come from people that look just like you. This may be shocking, but it is a reality that you may have to face. Some of our people have been beaten down for so long that they no longer believe in themselves and they most certainly don't believe in you. They buy into the myths about themselves and blacks in general. How is it that some of us have become so defeated? I'll share a story with you that was once shared with me.

A majestic elephant was captured from Africa to perform in an American circus. For years and years the elephant would try to escape, but the enormous chain around his ankle was so large that he could not break free. No matter how hard he tried, he could not overpower the massive chains. Eventually the elephant stopped trying to break free, because he had lost all desire. The circus owner found it no longer necessary to use large expensive chains to restrain the elephant and began to use just a small piece of rope around the elephant's ankle. This elephant had become so tired from resisting and so preoccupied with the repetitious tricks and routines of the circus that he never even noticed that his chains had been removed and replaced with something as flimsy as a cheap rope. The elephant remained a captive and continued to perform tricks for the circus until the day that he died. He never realized that there was very little holding him back after all.

Physical bondage was no longer the elephants' major problem, his major problem had become mental bondage. He could have easily broken a weak piece of rope, but he had given up because of all of his previous failed attempts to break free. Many of us have become the same way. We do not think that we can succeed and we remain defeated. The possibility of success does not seem real to us anymore. Even though the opportunity is here in America, many of us are so mentally defeated that we lack the confidence to try. Or we allow others that have no confidence in themselves to discourage us. They have started to believe all of the myths about us. Do not let these defeated people discourage you. After you break free, you can go back and free them.

On countless occasions after leaving the hospital, I have made stops at the gas station or the grocery store, taking care of my regular daily activities. Many times I've still had on my hospital scrubs and people will ask me what I do at the hospital. Almost never do people ever assume that I am a surgeon, even though at the time when they ask me this question I have on surgical attire. People make the assumption that I do everything except operate at the hospital. Once, while at the barber shop, I think I told a women five times in a row what I did for a living before it sunk in. Bear in mind that this was a black woman. Once again I was just leaving the hospital, and I was dressed in my all too familiar green pajamas, O.R. scrubs. The conversation went something like this.

Woman - "Do you work at the hospital?"
Me - "Yes"
Woman - "What do you do at the hospital?"
Me - "I operate"
Woman - "You work in the surgical department?"
Me - "Yes"
Woman - "What do you do?"
Me - "I operate."
Woman - "You work in the operating room?"
Me - "Yes"
Woman - "What do you do in the operating room?"
Me - "I operate"
Woman - "Are you some kind of surgical technician or something?"
Me - "No, I am a doctor"
Woman - "What kind of doctor are you?"
Me - "I am a surgeon."
Woman - "Oh that's nice. So you actually operate on people?"
Me - "Yes.

This conversation has happened more times than I care to remember. Unfortunately too many people, even some black people, still only see blacks in this country as 'the help' and not as the main ingredient. Unless we have the broom or mop in our hands we look out of place to some people, even our own people. Our youth need to understand that, in many instances, if they do not build a resume filled with academic success, the only thing that is waiting for them in the work place is the broom, the mop, or the funny-looking hamburger joint t-shirt. When this occurs, they will be fulfilling the roles that many Americans, black and white, have already envisioned for them.

CHAPTER 6

Why Are We So Far Behind?

I believe that to really understand where you want to go in life, you need to have a firm understanding of where you are starting from. I am from Detroit, born and raised there. If I wanted to go to Chicago, then knowing where Chicago is in respect to Detroit is very important, if I am to make a successful journey to Chicago. Chicago is 3-4 hours west of Detroit if you are traveling by automobile. If I was in Minnesota and started traveling west, I would never make it to Chicago. I would continue to drive until I fell into the Pacific Ocean. I would have wasted a lot of time, effort, and lots of money without ever reaching my desired destination. If I had set up a plan to get where I wanted to go, I would have been more successful and more effective along the way. If I had gotten a better understanding of where I was starting from, in relation to where I was going, it would have increased my chances of making it to my goal.

Where are you starting from? More than likely, you are starting from a disadvantaged situation when compared to the majority population. When I use the term majority and minority, I am referring to who is in control of the majority of the money, political power, and guns in this country. What do I mean when I say that you are probably starting from a disadvantaged background? I mean that the crime in your neighborhood is probably higher than the national average. The drug problem is probably evident in everyday life in your community. Lots of high school dropouts may surround you, and there is very little encouragement to go to school, nor do you see any benefits in your community from anyone going off to school. You probably know a handful of people under the age of 25 who have already passed away. A large proportion of these deaths are from violence and drug related activities. In my mind this is a disadvantaged background.

Living in circumstances such as these, how can children be convinced that education is important and is something that needs to be taken seriously? These same children see almost no benefit from education, although they have constantly been told about it in school. Solving algebra problems are far removed from a child's mind when these are the sights and sounds of his daily life. In my eyes this is a disadvantaged situation. A large segment of America's youth does not grow up like this. However, a large portion of the black population in America does grow up surrounded by conditions like this.

Since many of us start off in less than desirable living conditions, let's determine how we arrived at such dreadful conditions. About 400 years ago the first black slaves in this country arrived from West Africa. The people were used as free labor to toil the rich fertile soil of North America. The black slaves in this country were held in physical bondage and forced to work for free for over 200 years. Even after being set free from physical bondage after the abolishment of slavery, the blacks in this country were still in mental bondage and economic bondage. The effects of mental and economic bondage affected blacks long after the chains were removed.

After being released, they could not compete for well paying jobs because they were left ignorant and uneducated. Not to mention such direct attacks as things like Jim Crow laws. There was also a deep rooted prejudice against the ex-slaves that did not allow people to feel compassion for them or to treat them with respect. Because these people were former servants they were not treated as equals in society. From the time the slaves were brought to this country many people have allowed prejudice to dictate how they react towards blacks. Black men were considered to be only three-fifths of a man, not even equal to a whole man. Therefore, if the thought is that he was less than a man, then his mistreatment would be justified. The same way that few people feel remorse for caged animals, why feel remorse for a black man who is not even considered to be a whole man. Justified it was, as the slavery in this country treated blacks as worse than animals.

To tell someone that they are three-fifth's of a man is absolutely absurd. When these types of attitudes are displayed by some of the most respected members of the society it is easy to see how this mentality becomes shared by the people. Some of the so-called 'Founding Fathers' owned slaves themselves, and they were supposed to be our leaders. Prejudice and hate is not the only thing that kept black people behind. There was a very deliberate and direct attack on our education that also played an important role.

Teaching a slave to read or write during slavery was not allowed. When I first learned of this I was very young, and I did not understand the importance of such an action. I often asked myself, "What would it hurt to teach them to read and write?" I later discovered that knowledge is power. Power is something that is almost never surrendered. It is always taken. The slave masters knew that if the slaves were educated, they would quickly grow upset with their conditions and their status in this country. With knowledge, they would have the tools to better their situation. When you do not have knowledge, you are defenseless against many things in this world.

After the abolishment of slavery, the United States government promised every black man forty acres and a mule as a form of repayment and apology for mistreatment in this country. I want you to remember that wealth comes from ownership, please engrave that in your mind. You will never become wealthy working for someone else. Even today, land and real estate represent wealth and power all over the world. With the forty acres of land, and a mule to plow the land, black people would have been able to make wages for themselves and compete with whites in the cotton and tobacco industries. You must remember that black people, the ex-slaves, were the ones who had been plowing the fields for the last 200 years and had developed a definite mastery of the trade. The possibility of the slaves being set free, with there own land, would have left the whites with a severely depleted work force. This promise of forty acres and a mule was later rescinded and the ex-slaves were left with nothing. In a land that preaches fair competition, black people were denied that opportunity. Free, but unable to obtain work, many blacks were forced back to the plantations to do the same jobs they had been doing in the past but now with a label of free over their heads. In reality they were not free. They still depended on the majority population for their jobs that they received. This is not freedom. I challenge any black person reading this book. If you are on welfare, live in a housing project, or subsidized housing, or get any type of government aid, YOU ARE NOT FREE. As long as you depend on others for your daily needs, they dictate your life to you.

I would like to stop and focus on the forty acres and a mule for a moment. In this 'New Millennium' people don't want to hear about the promise of forty acres and a mule. They don't want to talk about what was done to black people in this country. People just want to be stroked and told that every thing is going to be all right and everything has a happy ending. Jewish people never let anyone forget what was done to them in the Holocaust. In the journey from Africa to America alone, it is estimated that more black people died than died in the entire Holocaust and we are afraid to speak up about it. We let people put a bug in our ear and tell us to 'get over it'. "That was hundreds of years ago," they say. You must understand that many things in your past can affect your future. We've let people convince us that slavery has no effect on the current situation. Many blacks in this country feel this way and want to believe that it has no relevance. People say that even though we weren't given the land and the mule it should not have held us back. I disagree.

Imagine this scenario. The year is 2003 and I own you. Literally I own you the way that you would own a dog. My family has owned your family for many generations now. I am wealthy and own a plant that manufactures small parts and distributes them to the automakers. I inherited this business from my father who inherited it from his father and so on. You have been an important part of my business for many years now and have become very good at your job. I have never taught you to read or write, I have only taught you how to help my business. You keep my assembly lines running and the products going out the door. Although you do good work and I make great profits, I pay you nothing for your labor. I personally supply you with everything that you need to live on. I feed you and I let you live on the grounds of my estate. You have a guest house in the back of my property. You drive to work in my car, because I don't pay you any money to purchase your own car.

Now the time has come for you to be free. The government has passed a law stating that I must release you. I have realized the sins of my grandfather. I recognize the evil acts that I committed against you and I am sorry. The remorse in my heart compels me to make an attempt to reward you, although I cannot truly repay you. Lost lives are never repaid, humans do not have that power, but at least I can give you something that can help you build a life for yourself and your children. This is what I will do. I will give you a warehouse of your own. I am also going to give you some shipping trucks to move your inventory from your warehouse to the desired destinations. You now have the resources to at least get started with. The bank may even give you a loan now since you have property, which is considered an asset. As expected, you are excited. You are about to be given the opportunity that you have always wanted. You will have your freedom and you plan to use it to its fullest extent. Then the bad news comes. All the things that I have promised you will be kept from you, except your freedom. You will not be receiving the warehouse that I promised you, nor will you receive the shipping trucks that I had promised you. But you still have your freedom. You are free to go and do whatever you want. So I tell you to go and still start a business. In your heart, you do have a desire to do so, but now you have no resources. You have no money, no property, and no collateral to get a loan. You can't even read the loan application at the bank. Do you think that the loan officer is going to give a loan to someone that can't even read the loan application? Do you think that the bank is going to give a loan to someone that doesn't have a job and doesn't have any collateral? Do you think that the bank will give a loan to someone that doesn't even have a bank account? What options do you have at this point?

This became the case for the freed slaves. Since it was illegal to teach them to read or write and they had been denied any resources to make their own living, they were forced back into the hands of people who did not even view them as a whole human being. If they did not go back to the plantation and work the fields, they would starve.

Besides the physical enslavement, black people were mentally enslaved as well. Mental defeat can be the hardest to overcome. This is the essence of what we are experiencing today. Thousands of blacks in this country walk around mentally defeated before they even get started.

How was the mental battle lost? Please respond to the following questions. How proud of yourself would you be if I kept chains on you and made you do all of the chores around my house and property? How would you feel at night when I went into my home to sleep in a warm soft bed while you slept outside in my barn on hay? When and if I ever allowed you to enter my home, you have to go through the back door because you are not good enough to enter through the front door. Even though you clean my home and do all of the chores, you are never paid for your work. At the same time I am making a handsome profit off of all the work that you do out in my fields. If at anytime you question my authority, I will tie you up and beat you with whips in front of your friends and family. If you try to escape from your conditions, I will catch you and I will tie rope around your neck and hang you from a tree until you die if I choose to. Even though I can beat you at anytime, it is criminal for you to strike me. How would you feel when I occasionally came into the barn at night to take your daughter, mother, or sister away for some sexual pleasure and then return her when I am done, the same way you return a video to Blockbuster when you are through with it? When I need some extra money, how does it feel when I take you downtown and stand you on a platform in front of half of the city inhabitants? As you stand there people bark out how much you are worth, "ONE THOUSAND, TWO THOUSAND, NO, NO, I'VE GOT THREE THOUSAND!" Are you feeling warm and fuzzy on the inside standing on the platform with those chains around your neck, wrists, and ankles? Years have gone by now, and the government says that I must release you. You are free to go now, go ahead and enjoy your life and hold your head up high. You have a lot to be proud of.

You sit patiently waiting for your forty acres and a mule that I have promised you but it never comes. You think to yourself, "Maybe I'll go to school and learn a trade or something." OOPS I forgot, I never taught you to read. Even if you could read, most schools would not allow your black skin to enter unless it was to mop the floor or take out the trash.

You start walking down the street wondering what your next move will be and how you will feed your family. You need time to clear your head and gather your thoughts. As you are walking down the street, you see me approaching and you quickly remember that you are not considered to be a man and you must step off of the sidewalk into the street or gutter to let me and my wife pass. That makes you feel good on the inside, doesn't it? You suddenly feel a stabbing pain in your stomach and hear a loud moaning sound. It is hunger calling you from the depths of your stomach and demanding to be satisfied. As you look up to the sky you see storm clouds coming and realize that you don't even own a home to protect yourself. While you were a slave, you lived on the master's property, but now you are free. You don't even have shelter for the night. You go and take refuge under a tree as the rain starts to pour down on your head and you begin to become soaked. The rain mixed with the wind causes chills to shake your limbs as your body gives its best attempt to keep itself warm by the rapid muscle contractions. At this moment you realize that you really have no options. You cannot feed or clothe yourself. You cannot read or write and you have no job. So you swallow your pride and go back to the master's home to ask if you can work in his field. Now you really feel free and independent don't you?

As the decades and years go by, your children, grandchildren, and great grandchildren gain very little more than what you had, because you've had nothing to pass down. They are not allowed to attend the same schools that the white children are allowed to attend. They are even told that they are not good enough to even drink from the same water fountains that the other children drink from. They are not allowed to sit at the counter of a diner and order a sandwich like everyone else. When they ride the bus, they are told that they must sit on the back of the bus because the front is reserved for the white people. Any time a black man stands up to say that we are being mistreated he is killed off to be shown as an example that complaining will not be tolerated. For a while you are not even allowed to compete in the same sports with everyone else.

After enduring centuries of this type of mistreatment, how can you expect someone to have a positive outlook on life? How can you expect someone to feel proud about themselves? It is not going to happen. Unless we look past this small segment of history and learn our true origin and source. When I was in history class in high school, the only section of the book that talked about Africa was the section on slavery, and it showed a picture of a black man with a bone through his nose. There is so much more to us than the segment of time that we were slaves in this country. God did not create you to be a second class citizen. That is not his purpose for your life.

I believe that we are now offered unprecedented opportunities for success in America. We must take advantage of these opportunities. I believe that being armed with your God-given talents, combined with 100% effort, and refusing to give up, a young black child in America can grow to be whatever they desire to be. I do not believe that there is anything in this world that can stop you if you try hard enough.

These things should not stir up hate in your heart but should motivate you to come up with a plan to change your circumstances. I did not share these things with you for you mope or feel sorry for yourself. Don't believe that you cannot do what you want because you were born poor. Educate yourself and develop a plan to break the cycle of poverty and ignorance that permeates our neighborhoods. I shared these things with you to remind you not to fall into the same predicament and to show you that being free is not enough. When you are uneducated you are at the mercy of others. No matter how free you are physically, if you are uneducated, you will experience very little of the richness that this life has to offer.

CHAPTER 7

OUR BLAME

"And why beholdest thou the mote that is in thy brother's eye, but considereth not the beam that is in thine own eye?"

-Jesus the Christ

Often when people are trying to find a solution to a problem they spend a lot of time arguing and blaming others for the situation. When the finger pointing starts, we rarely stop to point some of those fingers at ourselves and determine how much of the blame is our own. Yes, we do share some blame for our lack of education and our lack of success. So who exactly is to blame among us? It is time for some honesty.

For myself, when I want to determine who has been the chief

architect for the failures and troubles in my life, I take a short walk to the bathroom and look in the mirror. When I have gotten into trouble in the past it was because of stupid things that I did, not what someone made me do. When I did not do well in endeavors in the past, it was because I did not apply myself properly and did not work hard enough. It was not because I couldn't do the work. Where you are today is due to decisions that you have made in the past. Whether you are doing well or not so well, a major determinant of your position right now is due to decisions that you have made in the past. I am fully aware of our history in this country, but that is no excuse for not succeeding today in America. I did not say that things would not be harder for you when compared to other groups. I am certainly not saying that. There is no question that your road to success may be much more difficult when compared to other races. Your access to resources may be limited at times, but it will not be impossible. If I never reach my dreams, I am the only person that I can blame for that.

If we are honest with ourselves, anyone who has not achieved their goals can look at things that they did wrong to contribute to their own downfall. It may have been hanging with the wrong crowd and too much drinking and partying in high school. The wrong decisions about sex may have caused a pregnancy that deterred us. Pure laziness may have been our downfall in some cases. Not listening to authority figures and the advice that they provide hurts many people. A lot of times listening to other people's negative talk discourages us. If we all look back over our lives, we can find countless errors in judgment that have deterred our success.

Every successful black person from the ghetto that has not shown others (besides their own children) to duplicate their success has to share some blame. We must escape the "I got mine, now you get yours mentality." The 'each one teach one' concept can be very helpful if more of us adopted this creed. We must stop looking to others outside of our race to supply our help and needs. We have successful people in our own communities that can be examples on how to achieve. I am not saying that successful people should still live in the projects. You should be able to live in the most beautiful, safest home that your money can afford. But when our own are able to break away from the pack and never look back with any compassion or advice, how can we expect others to feel the need to help? I personally will find no joy in my success if I haven't helped someone else along the way.

Even the failures among us are valuable. These experiences can be priceless lessons of what not to do to the young and impressionable minds of our youth. Don't just sit there and watch someone fall into the same hole that you did, warn them. Don't be so ashamed that you cannot share your mistakes. We can all learn a lot from each other.

Parents that don't take a proper role in their child's education are to blame for the lack of our success. I have heard many horrendous stories from my teacher-friends regarding these issues. I have been told stories about parents complaining that their child is being given too much homework. In my opinion, there is no such thing as too much homework. You can never have too much homework. When parents project this lazy attitude, how dare we expect the children to be motivated to excel. You can bench press a five-pound weight everyday for years and it will not make you stronger. If you do not stress and exercise your brain, it will not become strong. Your brain is the biggest muscle in your body and it must be challenged and worked daily in order for you to advance beyond your current circumstances.

Every politician and public official that thinks that it is more important to build stadiums, casinos, and smoother roads shares the blame if these things come before properly educating our children.

Every educator that allows lies to be spread to our children shares some blame for our lack of academic success. Christopher Columbus DID NOT DISCOVER AMERICA. You cannot discover something that is already inhabited. How ridiculous would it be for me to show up in your backyard next weekend at your barbecue and say "Look what I discovered, new territory"? It sounds foolish doesn't it? But we allow foolishness to be passed on to our children, and we don't even question the material. Later on when our children learn that they have been deceived it erodes their faith in the education system. When I realized that many things I had been forced to learn were lies, it made me believe that education was not important, and it was a pack of worthless lies, and I was just wasting my time. Had I continued in this thinking I would not be where I am today.

I had completely lost faith in academics at one point. Simply due to the lies that I had been told. I felt betrayed by those that I thought were there to lead and guide me. A course like American History is a required course to get a high school diploma in the state of Michigan. Many of today's youth, that I have come into contact with, feel the exact same way. They believe that education adds absolutely no value to their life and does not add any potential to their future. It is so difficult to convince them otherwise when they find out some of these things are flat-out untrue.

Inspect your child's history book. The one that we used had about one paragraph or so about black history in America and it only mentioned the slavery aspect. I was so disgusted and disappointed in our system and society when I found out that we have contributed so much more to this world and very few of our educators in the public school system are brave enough to speak up and say it. No one had the courage to say that the Christopher Columbus story was not being correctly told. No one had the courage to say that the original inhabitants of this country were deceived and removed by tricks and by force. In some Hollywood movies, the natives of this country are painted as savages. What would your response be if I moved on to your property and decided I was going to have it for myself? You would probably defend yourself with force.

This caused me to lose faith in our system, and I started to believe that everything was just a big lie. I didn't feel the need to be in school because I would just be lied to even more and how could these lies benefit me? People that know the truth are sometimes afraid to say it and children can be scarred by it.

There is another area where I think that we have to shoulder some of the blame. All too often many of our young children attempt a blueprint for success that has already failed someone that has gone ahead of them. If dropping out of high school and taking a job at a local factory didn't bring much success for your uncle, then why would you do the exact same thing? If you have an older brother that has been incarcerated or killed while participating in the drug business, then why would you take the same path? If your older sisters have had children without a husband and it has led her away from school and success, then why would you fall into the same trap after seeing that this pathway brings no success? If you are riding down a one way street with a dead end then you should turn around. Especially if you have already seen someone crash. Don't tell yourself that you can make that pathway work, instead choose another path that has already been proven to be successful.

As a teenager, I had many of the above situations in my life. I had family members who were killed while participating in the drug game. I had family members who died from drug overdoses. I had family members with multiple babies and no husband. Many of my family members have dropped out of school, and no one in my family had ever gone to college. I have family members that have been in and out of jail. There were gangs in my neighborhood, and I knew people that would bring guns to school. I saw all of the above situations around me for many years. While seeing all of these things, one thing that I did not see was success being the result of any of the above actions. It was clearly obvious to me that none of the above actions was allowing anyone to retire early and travel the world.

Even before I ever felt that college was an option for me I did know that it would do me no good at all to follow the same pathway as some of the people that had gone before me. Even though I didn't know what the right path was, I definitely knew what the wrong path was. In a multiple choice exam, sometimes just knowing the wrong answers can help you narrow things down. This is not to say that I have not made any mistakes either. I have made plenty of mistakes and have made my share of poor decisions. What I have tried to do with my mistakes was learn from my ignorance and poor decision making and be sure not to go down that path again.

Thinking back on my old neighborhood, there are many things that occurred that can be looked at as a direct influence on our lack of success. What are some other ways that we have hampered our own success? In my old neighborhood I never saw a white man running a crack house. I have never seen a white man selling marijuana in my old neighborhood. The gangs in my neighborhood were all black. Don't give me those lines about who owns the planes that flies the drugs and guns into our neighborhoods. I know all that stuff. The ultimate decision still lies with us. We must become accountable for our own actions and decisions. Just because someone supplies us with our own tools for destruction, it does not mean that we have to accept them and then use them against each other. We must start to make smarter decisions. When the bullets ring out in our black neighborhoods, black men are most often pulling the triggers. When I am in the emergency rooms and bruised and battered black women come in, most often black men have abused them.

No one holds us down and forces all of the alcohol down our throats. When my home was broken into, it was black men from my neighborhood that did it. It was black men that murdered my cousins.

We willingly step up and volunteer to sell and use drugs. No one makes us do that. We have to take the blame for some of our own demise. When we focus more time on making sure our child has the latest shoes, rather than making sure that he understands his homework, we share some of the blame. When we put more money into alcohol, cigarettes, and lottery tickets, than saving for our children's tuition, then we share some of the blame. When we don't support our teachers and only show up at school ready to fight them and argue with them, we share some of the blame.

We should never forget what was done to our people. There is no question that a tremendous injustice has been done to blacks in this country. No one can deny that fact. If anyone tries to deny it, then they are fooling themselves or they are being plain dishonest. It is not just the initial injustice that has affected us but also the continued disrespect and unfair treatment for over one-hundred years following the abolishment of slavery. At the same time, we must move forward. We cannot stay with our minds frozen in time and constantly blaming our lack of success on what has been done to us. We must pick ourselves up from where we are right now and move forward. We must use whatever tools we have at our disposal to gain access to the areas that our people so desperately need. We must become educated in all areas, not just a fancy university education.

Unfortunately because of what has happened to us, it has sent some of us into a perpetual mode of blaming other people for each and every ill that affects our community. The more time we focus on blaming others, the less time we have to focus on changing our own situations. As long as everything is somebody else's fault, we will be less likely to focus on a plan to change our conditions. Do not allow anyone to convince you that you should forget your past. No one ever tells Jewish people to forget about the holocaust. Don't ever forget, but don't allow it to be a crutch either. Let's start changing some of our own self-destructive behaviors.

It is a common theme in the black community to discuss what someone is doing to us. The more we empower ourselves the less people will be able to do to us. Educating ourselves is a form of empowerment. When we remain ignorant to certain things we remain vulnerable. Until we become more financially savvy we will remain vulnerable. As long as we still pay $200 for a video game before we have $200 in a mutual fund, we will remain vulnerable. As long as we devote more time to the television than we do to books and education, we will remain vulnerable.

It is a hard pill to swallow sometimes but we need to wake up. Every unsuccessful person has made a significant contribution to his or her lack of success. We must be honest with ourselves and start to change those things that are hindering us from our own success.

CHAPTER 8

MENTORS

"He that walketh with wise men shall be wise: but a companion of fools shall be destroyed"

-King Soloman

I just have a few words to say about mentors. Be careful about how you choose the people that will be giving advice to you. This is very difficult sometimes because many people offer up advice without even being asked or having the experience to correctly comment on your situation. If there is one thing that people do not mind giving away, it is their opinion.

There are some scenarios where people are actually paid to give advice. At some universities, each student is assigned an advisor. An advisor is someone that you can go and talk to for advice on course selection and career choices. You should always take this advice and compare it with what you feel in your heart, because you will have to live with your decisions for the rest of your life. You must also be wise enough to compare advice from different sources. Do not believe that only one person has the answer to all of your questions. You should also be aware that all advisors do not have your best interests in mind, and any person that is not considerate of what you want for your future is not the person for you. Some advisors try to push you into their field because it is what they enjoy, but it may not be what you enjoy.

Do not be discouraged by advisors who tell you that you can't do it or that you should choose another field. While in college, I shared an advisor with one of my future medical school classmates. I can remember telling my classmate about my first meeting with this advisor. I walked into his office and sat down, we shook hands and began to talk. His first question was, "What do you want to do?"

I told him that I wanted to go to medical school.
He opened up my file, looked at my GPA and said,
"What else do you want to do?"
I said, "Huh?"
He said, "What are you going to do if you don't get in?"
I said, "I don't know, I really don't want to do anything else."
"Well you need to start thinking about it because you probably won't make it."

I couldn't believe it. How could he be so flat out and cold about it? What if I also wasn't sure if I could make it and needed an extra push of encouragement? He sure wasn't looking to provide it. I will admit that at that time in my academic career that my GPA was not stellar, but I wasn't even a sophomore in college yet and needed still close to 100 credits to graduate. 100 credits away and he's telling me to hang it up! For those of you who are not in college or have never taken college courses, these courses are 3-4 credits per class, so 100 credits is years away from graduation. Instead of saying, "Well Roderick, first we need to work on your grades. Medical schools like to see their candidates with higher GPA's. Next you should start doing some volunteer work at the local hospitals. If you have some free time you should get involved in a research project in something that interests you." He attempted to destroy my dreams before they even got started. After that day, I have never gone to see that man again.

My medical school classmate that I was discussing this with actually did research for this person in his lab. When it was close to graduation time he told her that she shouldn't go to medical school and that she should get her Ph.D. instead. Why he chose to inflict his selfish motives on her is beyond my understanding, but he has definitely established a pattern of this type of behavior. The bottom line is that all advisors do not have your best interest in mind.

When I first realized that I wanted to be surgeon I thought that I wanted to be a trauma surgeon. These types of doctors do emergency surgery on sometimes critically ill people after severe injuries such as gun shots and auto accidents. Thinking that this would be my path in life, I sought out a trauma surgeon for a mentor. I was aggressive in my approach, and this man didn't know me from anywhere. I tracked down his pager number and paged him out of the blue. I told him that I wanted to be a surgeon and would like to work in his research lab. He said no problem, and I worked for him the summer between my first and second years of medical school. Over the next few years I participated in other projects with him and even did my third year surgery clerkship with him. During that same time I started leaning towards becoming an orthopaedic surgeon instead of a trauma surgeon.

Early in my fourth year of medical school, I had finalized my decision to become an orthopaedic surgeon as opposed to a trauma surgeon. When I told him that I had changed my mind what do you think he did? He went to the chairman of the department of Orthopaedic Surgery and gave him a verbal personal recommendation for me on the spot. I don't mean a couple of weeks later but about fifteen minutes later he did this for me. Although he was disappointed that I did not go into his field, he did not let that cloud his judgment. This is the type of mentor/advisor that you need on your side.

I was very persistent when attempting to meet this surgeon. Why? Because he was already at a place that I wanted to be at one day. My persistence paid off.

A classmate of mine was related to an orthopaedic surgeon. When I was just considering this field, I needed to talk with someone to learn more about it and get some guidance. I probably called his home maybe nine or ten times over the course of a few months until I was finally able to speak with him. Sometimes I would call as late as 11:00 at night trying to reach him, because I knew what I wanted and I went for it. He could have either said yes or no, period, but it would not have been the end of the world. Fortunately he didn't say no and I received a lot of helpful advice from him.

The very worse he could have done was to tell me that he was unwilling to help me. This is not the big deal that people make it out to be. You know what I have noticed after people tell me no? What I have noticed is that I am still breathing, the sun is still shining, and life goes on. It is not the end of the world.

I am a pest when it comes to trying to position myself where I want to be. Wherever you want to go, you need to talk to someone that is already there. I bug people, yet they have always been very polite, and no one has lost their patience with me yet. I am really persistent with people when it comes to my success. I cannot rest until I know the right answer to my problem. At almost every turn I am calling and calling and calling. I am bouncing scenarios off of people and constantly asking for other contacts and information. I act this way because I understand the importance of mentors for success.

Another reason why I act this way is because I understand the importance of what I am trying to do. It will not only benefit me, but there are others around me that will also reap the rewards. I refuse to be lazy when is comes to my future. I think that there is a lot of truth to the statement, 'only the strong survive'. In our society, the weak are not necessarily killed off, but they are subject to do the bidding of others. Think of your education as the foundation of what can literally effect you for the rest of your life. It can have an effect on where you work, how much money you make, other business opportunities etc., so you should take it very seriously. You may need to hunt down some of the people that you will need to work in your favor. Trust me, it will be well worth it.

Even as a surgeon during my training period I had older surgeons who mentored me in the proper care of patients. The day that I graduated from medical school I was a doctor. Even though I had the title of M.D. behind my name I had very little of the skills necessary to perform complex operations and manage detailed patient care. How did I rectify this deficiency in my abilities and knowledge? I corrected my weaknesses by allowing myself to be guided by surgeons that already possessed the skills and abilities that I was attempting to gain.

The very first step in choosing a mentor is discovering where you as an individual want to go. What are you trying to accomplish? Do you want to open your own business? Do you want to be an engineer?

After you determine what you want to do, the next step is to find someone that is already doing what you want to be doing in the future. Be very polite but also be very persistent. Go up to that person or write that person or do whatever you have to do to get in contact with that person. Ask them if it would be possible for them to have a conversation with you about your goals and ask them if they would be willing to guide you in some manner. Some of these people are going to say no. Do you think that this has stopped me? Well obviously not if I am writing this book on how to become successful. If they say no, then move on to the next person, count it as a loss for them.

People love admiration. Everyone enjoys the idea that someone else thinks highly of them. Remember this and it may help you conquer any fear that you may have about going up to speak to a total stranger. When you tell most people that there is a facet of their life that you admire and would like to pattern yourself after, most people will be very happy to assist you. Most will be honored that someone feels that way about them.

So, now you've found a potential mentor and they've agreed to speak with you at some time, what's next? I will share one of the tactics that I use to put people at ease. I invite them out to lunch or dinner. The meal is on me of course. I pay the whole bill. We don't go to some burger joint, but we go somewhere that they like or a nice restaurant that I choose. Remember, this is your future, and you cannot afford to be cheap. Why do I do this? Because the knowledge that I obtain from this meeting will pay me thousands of dollars more than what the meal will cost me. When I apply the knowledge that I obtained from the meeting it will make me more money than I spent many times over. Another powerful tool is that I can write the whole meal off as a tax-deductible business expense because I own companies.

Knowledge is power people. This is how the rich get richer. So while you expend your funds on the same priced meal as me, I am allowed to obtain a refund from the government as a business expense. This is in addition to all of the knowledge that my dinner guest (possible future mentor) just shared with me which will pay dividends for decades to come. Life is not about working harder, it is about working smarter. Use the strongest muscle in your body, your brain, to move the world.

Muhammad Ali, 'The Greatest' as he is sometimes called, had a trainer. Someone that saw what he couldn't see. He had someone that could guide him and advise him. All the great athletes have coaches. Raw talent is not enough. You need to meet and talk with people that can guide you and steer you in the proper direction. They will have insight that only comes from years of experience.

What if you can't find a mentor that can sit and talk with you? There are people that have influenced me that I have never met. I love reading, and I read books all of the time. When I realized that books, not television, had the answers to my questions on how to become successful, I was hooked on books. You can go to a bookstore and find a book on almost any subject that interests you. Let's dispel the myth that if you want to hide something from a black person just put it in a book. Successful people read all of the time. Not only do they read all the time, but the content of what they read is going to strengthen them. They don't spend a lot of time on the sports section or the funny papers. Because very little in these sections is going to give you the ammunition that you need to become successful. Take the approach that if it is not going to make me better, then I don't need it.

Ok, now that you have gotten tons of advice from your mentors, what's next? This is the easy part, just do it. Many people know what they should be doing but few people are actually doing it. Knowledge is useless unless you apply it to your life. What good does it do you to know that you should stop at a red light if you are going to go right through it? It does you absolutely no good at all.

Application plays a very important part in your success. As a matter of fact, I suggest that it is mandatory for your success. You can learn all of the things necessary for success, but if you don't apply them then you will not have benefited. You must apply what you have learned, because just having information isn't going to cut it.

Do not allow these encounters with your possible mentors to be one time meetings or occasional occurrences. By staying in touch with them it allows them to assess your progress and maybe divert your course if you start to faint or sway from the path of success. It allows them to keep tabs on you and advise you if changes need to be made.

CHAPTER 9

CONSIDER THE FARMER

"For Whatsoever a Man Soeth, That Shall he also Reap"
-The Apostle Paul

The farmer is a very interesting figure in American society. He doesn't come to mind when our children start to consider careers and future endeavors. The farmer never makes the front page of Ebony or Jet magazine. He never makes the cover of Black Enterprise magazine. Although he is an obscure figure in our society, he lives his life in a way that can have a tremendous impact on all of us. What we need to understand is that there are a lot of things that we can learn from the farmer. Let's take a look.

First, the farmer has a very strong work ethic. There are not many people that can outwork a farmer. He gets up very early in the morning before the sun comes up and he works all day.

Ask any surgeon that has ever worked in a VA hospital how he feels about farmers. VA hospitals are government-run hospitals that provide health care to veterans of the armed forces. Of all their patients, many surgeons will tell you that they enjoy the farmers the most. Why? They make no excuses and they ask no favors. If they have an eight o'clock appointment, they are sitting in the lobby at seven o'clock A.M. Many of these guys drive two and three hours to get to their appointment.

Notice how long you have driven outside of a big city before you start to see farms with hundreds of animals on it. You can drive many many miles outside of the city before you see these places. This is where these guys come from to get to a doctor in the city. Do they complain? Not a bit. I have met patients that have had to get on the road at three or four in the morning to make it to a surgery that is scheduled for seven or eight in the morning.

When it is all over, what do these guys say to you? "Thanks doc!" It really amazes me how these guys are so much alike, almost across the board. Let's look a little deeper into why we brought up the life of the farmer. I want you to really pay attention to his lifestyle because if you adopt many of the principles that the farmer lives by it will bless you tremendously.

One of the farmer's greatest assets is how he lives his life. His whole existence is based on the premise of sowing and reaping. His entire livelihood is based on this. The farmer plants a particular crop and after adequate nurturing he expects a harvest. Because he has sown, he expects to reap. Success is not an accident, remember that.

The farmer knows that if he plants corn in the right soil, at the right time, and if the corn gets the right amount of water and the right amount of sunlight, a harvest will come. The harvest is the collective results of all of his hard work. The harvest that he collects from his planted seeds can do so many things for him. The harvest can feed his family. If he so chooses, he can sell part of his harvest for money. The money that he receives from selling part of his harvest can be used to purchase more seed which can be planted to produce another harvest. This cycle of sowing and reaping can be a continuous flow for this farmer and his family.

You can be this successful or even more so without ever driving a tractor. Not by learning agriculture in depth but by just learning how to plant seeds. It is a very simple, yet very powerful concept. Whatsoever a man soeth, that shall he also reap.

Many times we look around and are shocked by the fact that we don't have as much money as we would like or that we don't have a successful career. This confuses many of us and we sit around and wonder why. Why aren't things going better than this for me? The answer is very simple, but many of us just don't focus on the concept. If you want to know why you are where you are today, all you have to do is look back at the seeds that you've planted in the past.

People ask themselves, why am I still in this dead end job? Well think back and tell me what kind of different seeds you have planted in the past year to give you a different harvest. What specific moves have you made--real action, in the last year to remove you from this dead end job? Just talking about it is not going to be enough. You know what a lot of us will do? A lot of us will get up every morning and do the same thing day after day. We follow the same routine month after month still expecting different results. We complain about how bad things are, but we do absolutely nothing to change it.

I have encountered similar scenarios when talking to people about debt. People amaze me when they tell me that they are trying to get out of debt but admit that they haven't changed their spending habits. It doesn't make any sense, but this is what we do. We continue to plant the same seeds but say that we would like a different harvest. You cannot plant apple seeds and honestly expect to get oranges when it is time for the harvest.

If you plant seeds of laziness then you can expect a harvest of poverty. Your harvest will never be greater than the seeds that you have planted. So you say that you want to be successful? You say that you want success to be your harvest? What kinds of seeds have you planted to bring about this harvest? You can't sleep until noon everyday and expect to have a flourishing career in something. Your investment strategy can't be lottery tickets and the casinos and expect wealth to be your harvest.

Just having possession of seeds is not good enough either. I can keep a pack of seeds in my pocket for years, and I promise you that nothing will grow from these seeds. So many of us are walking around with wonderful ideas in our heads. These ideas will not do us any good if we choose not to act on them. Those seeds in your mind cannot grow if you don't plant them. Those ideas in your head are no better than the seeds that I have left in my pocket. There will be no growth at all if seeds are not planted.

Have you ever seen someone become successful at something that you once considered doing? I think that most of us have been there. We've been in the grocery store or the mall and we've seen a product selling like hot cakes that we'd thought about selling years ago. The difference is that someone actually acted on what you knew would be a great idea. Seeds are no good unless planted.

Your seeds have to be planted in the right place also. What kind of harvest do you think that I would have if I took a pack of seeds and threw all the seeds out on the concrete? My harvest would be nothing. Right? The birds would love me, but I would get absolutely nothing in return. You must be careful where you plant your seeds if you ever expect to get a harvest.

Many people will tell you that they have been planting seeds for years and have not seen a return. Well where do you plant them? Do you plant your seeds in the lottery line and expect wealth? Why do people believe this? Where is the evidence that this brings financial stability? Where is the evidence that playing the black jack table will bring financial security? But these are the places where many of us will plant our seeds. The strangest part is not that this is where we plant the seed. The strangest part is that we really expect a harvest from it without having seen other farmers get a harvest from it.

If I stand one-hundred farmers in a line and they all plant

apple seeds, I am very confident that there will be a bountiful harvest of apples to come. Next, you can line up one-hundred people in the lottery line, and they can place bets from birthdays, dream books, numbers, or whatever source they like. In most cases, none of them will obtain financial security as a harvest from the seeds that they are planting. So if you already know that laying seeds out on the concrete gets you nothing, it is probably not an activity that should be continued. You reap what you sow.

Are you planting seeds for success or are you planting seeds for failure? If you sit up and watch television all day what kind of harvest do you expect this to produce? Do you expect success to come from this? Of course not. So if it doesn't produce success then why put such a large portion of your time (seeds) into it? You reap what you sow.

Do you spend lots of your time on the telephone having meaningless conversations about this and about that? How many of these seeds of your time have you planted in conversations about uplifting yourself and your family and your community? We give a lot of lip service to these issues, but how much action do we really show?

Maintaining a proper environment for your seeds is equally important. After a farmer plants his seeds he doesn't go on vacation and come back many months later when it is time to reap. The farmer tends to his seeds, his investment, on a regular basis to make sure that the appropriate environment for success is maintained. He understands that just planting seeds is not enough and he must perform active maintenance to ensure that his seeds are not eaten by the birds. He must spray pesticide to kill pests and make sure weeds do not choke his crops. Without proper maintenance of the environment around his seeds, he will be unsuccessful.

Another important concept that we must learn from the farmer is the season. Each harvest only comes in due season. Some of us can be so impatient at times. We want it all right now. If I can't have it right now, then I don't want it at all. The farmer doesn't plant his seeds on a Monday and then expects to reap his harvest the following Monday. The farmer understands that it takes time for his seeds to grow.

A lot of people are discouraged from becoming a surgeon because it takes so long and requires many years of school. I am a surgeon today because of the seeds that I planted in the past. Now it is the season for my harvest. I planted those seeds over ten years ago, by passing my pre-medical courses in college. My harvest came years later. Most of us want a big harvest but are not willing to wait for our due season for our harvest to come.

Most of the things in my life that I am currently enjoying are a result of seeds previously planted. We must master this concept. The seeds that you plant today will determine your harvest in the future. Part of the draw of the lottery and the casino is the instant gratification and the potential rush that comes along with the possibility of instant wealth. It is not exciting when you learn that proper investing will make you wealthy. It is not appealing because it requires a season, or waiting period, for it to come to pass. There is a waiting period required before we can enjoy this harvest.

If most of us could just get past the lure of instant gratification, it would be such a large step towards our goals of success. Everything has a season, even success. We are too impatient to wait on success, yet we rush to destruction. Because we are so impatient, we get ourselves into huge mountains of credit card debt. Because we just have to have it right now, we charge, and we charge, and we charge. It causes us to pay three times as much as we should be paying for something, all because of our impatience. Six months later we are still paying for an item and we see something else that we just have got to have and there we go charging again, all the while accumulating more and more debt. Be mindful of the concept of the season. Plant your seeds in fertile ground, maintain it and wait for it to grow.

This impatience is a major factor in why many of our black youth participate in the drug game. The idea of fast money, 'the I must have it now mentality', has sent more of our young men to an early grave than I care to think about. If you can just hold out and wait for your season after planting your seeds in fertile ground, I promise you that it will be well worth the wait.

A farmer lives his life by planting seeds and waiting for a harvest. How successful do you think he would be if he ate all of his seeds? Let's take it to another level. He was so greedy that he not only ate all of his seeds, he ate more seeds than he had. He went next door to the next farm and borrowed seeds and ate all of those borrowed seeds as well. Do you think we will see this guy on the cover of MONEY Magazine for his in-depth financial knowledge? Of course not, that guy is going broke fast. Not only will he be broke fast, he'll end up starving. If he eats all of his seeds, what will the farmer plant? What will his children eat?

It is easy to see the consequences of these scenarios when they apply to other people's lives. We rarely take a step back to evaluate our own life. It is just so much easier to pick and find fault in everyone else. This scenario of eating all the seeds is played out in every black neighborhood in America.

Some of us get a paycheck (potential seeds) and spend every last nickel. Not only do we spend every last nickel, some of us spend more than we make. We can spend more money than we make by borrowing more money to spend by using lots of credit cards. We eat every last seed until it is gone. Some of us don't even put a small portion of it to the side for a future harvest. I think that most of you would agree that a farmer that eats all of his seeds is not a smart farmer. This is a farmer destined for poverty. We cannot continue to eat (spend) every single seed that we get our hands on. We must plant a portion of the seeds for a future harvest.

A percentage of every dollar that you receive should be invested (planted) into some form of investment vehicle. Someone is going to say, "But I don't know how to invest." So what, go find someone that does know how to invest (plant seeds). When farmers are born do they know how to plant crops? No, they learn from another farmer.

And don't just talk to people who know how to invest, turn the TV off and go to the bookstore and educate yourself on money and investments. It is time to plant seeds, tend to your fields, and wait for your harvest.

There are many things that you have that can be considered a seed. Your time is a seed. Your finances are potential seeds. Both of these, when used wisely, can produce a bountiful harvest for you. Time is more valuable than you think, so don't waste it. You don't have as much time as you think that you have. You should spend the majority of your time doing things that are going to improve your life, not make it worse or keep it the same. Plant your seeds (time) into harvest-producing areas. People tell me that they could not have gone to school for as long as I did, but I was planting seeds all of those years with my time. I used my time to focus on something that would bring me a harvest. Over that same period of time that I was in school, many people did nothing but work dead-end jobs, not gaining any success. So why not use all those years to plant seeds? We can be so backwards at times. "That's going to be too much work, I can't do that." Well what are you going to do instead? "I don't know, but I'll figure something out." Ten years later, still no harvest but still complaining about not being where we think that we should be.

If you are really serious about changing your circumstances then I want you to perform a simple exercise. Get a vivid picture in your mind of exactly where you want to be in life. Be very specific with this, no generalizations. Don't just write down, 'I want a whole bunch of money', be very specific. After you have it written down, put it in a drawer on your desk. For the next week I want you to keep a diary of your daily activities. Write down where you went, for how long, what you read and what you watched on television. After a week, pull out that piece of paper that you wrote your goals on and compare it with your diary of activities for the previous week. Try to see if what you did for that last week were seeds planted towards your goals. This will give you a better understanding of how to plant towards your specific harvest. Your activities must become goal-oriented. Not just mundane activities that you participate in just because your friend invited you. You must start to ensure that your activities are specifically intended to get you closer to your goal of success. If you find tasks on that piece of paper that have absolutely nothing to do with where you are trying to go, then your daily agenda needs to change.

So the next time you are on the road traveling to another state don't look at those fields of crops the same. Remember that the farmer, his lifestyle, and the principles that he lives by can make a tremendous difference in your life.

CHAPTER 10

PROPER ENVIRONMENT FOR SUCCESS

To me, plant life is one of God's most amazing creations. As humans we require oxygen in the right concentrations to survive. It must be a component of our environment in order for us to survive. Green plants make the oxygen that we need to live, while they live on the carbon dioxide that we release as waste products. We share an awesome relationship with plants and most of us rarely consider it. Our environment is in constant exchange from one group to the next and this is very important for growth. Without the proper exchange within the environment, we wouldn't have the proper living conditions required for growth and survival. The right mixture of the appropriate ingredients is essential.

Plants require the proper mixture in their environment in order for them to survive and blossom. They require certain amounts of sunlight and water, as well as proper temperatures in order to survive. When the proper environment is not provided for a plant the chances for its survival starts to decrease. When proper maintenance is not provided for plant life weeds can come in and destroy a beautiful garden. Do not allow certain weeds of life to come and choke out your dreams of success. You have to be ever so conscious of your environment and the people around you. If you are not rooted in the proper environment, it will be very difficult to achieve your dreams and goals. If you do not perform proper maintenance on your environment, certain weeds (people) will come and choke the life right out of your dreams. You must constantly tend to your garden (environment) where you have planted your seeds for success. Constant proper maintenance to remove any pests or weeds that may halt the growth of your harvest is a must.

There are many traps and pitfalls that deters many black youth from the path of success. The obstacles are countless and some of our children stumble over them so often that it starts to appear as if they are almost aiming for them intentionally. Because these traps appear to snare some of them on such a regular basis, many people start to expect failure for our children and become surprised by their success when it occurs. Patients still do double takes sometimes when I open their doors and meet them for the first time.

Growing up black in this country most often means a greater possibility of being surrounded by drugs and crime. It has become a pervasive part of our community and the environment around us. You may be hard-pressed to find a black person that was born and raised in a major city in this country that has not personally been touched by drugs in some way, shape or form. Drugs and drug-related crimes have penetrated almost every aspect of our society whether directly or indirectly. You do not have to be a sociologist to see the effects on the people around us. We see it on the news or hear the stories everyday from our friends and co-workers. The stories of the crack-addicted mothers who bring crack-addicted children into the world. The senseless murders that occur over drug deals gone bad or control over drug territory. We hear about the innocent people that are shot down by stray bullets during drive-by shootings. It has become so common that most of us are no longer shocked by it. It doesn't surprise us like it use to, we have become desensitized to it.

I have been personally affected by drugs, even though I have never sold a crack vial. My older cousin was a drug dealer. He was shot in the back four times by people that he knew. He received a phone call one morning and he told the person on the other end that he would be there shortly. He left to go and meet this person and no one ever saw him alive again. He was found in a field with four bullets in his back. He had a Mercedes-Benz, a Corvette, and mink coats, but the end result of his life was nothing. I had a female cousin that overdosed on drugs and died, cousins that have been in and out of jail multiple times for drugs or other crime related activities. With distractions like these, you can see how the last thing on some of our children's minds would be square roots and equations. So in the midst of this, how are you supposed to obtain success in life? Let's analyze the situation further.

First, let's talk about why many of our youth choose crime verses education and do a comparison of the two paths. I think that the first thing we have to look at is environment. Children from educated families/environments are more likely to go to college than children from uneducated families/environments. Very simply stated, sometimes it is very easy to believe in something that we have seen with our own eyes. Unless we are very conscious of our actions, it is very easy for us to become what we see. If we come from neighborhoods were no one is educated then we have no one to pattern ourselves after for academic success. If no one around a small child is educated or even speaks or encourages education then where will the motivation to obtain an education come from? There's no one to explain to the child the importance of education and give tangible examples to prove that it is the correct path to take. Some children can't just be told that education is the right choice, they have to be shown that it is the right choice. At the same time, if we come from neighborhoods where there are plenty of drug dealers with big wads of cash, then we have plenty of people to show us an example of how to obtain fast money.

To contrast the path of education, these young men and the women that date them, show our children many tangible examples as to why school is not the best path to take. Many of our youth that have chosen the path of selling drugs live in better homes and handle more money than our parents have ever had in their lifetimes. They can afford all the material items that our children crave. They appear to be having so much fun at the same time, all without having to go to school. The girls involved are seen in the best cars with the dealers and they are taken to the best restaurants and they are wearing the best clothes. Why go to school when I can have all of my heart's desires without having to do homework, listen to my teachers, or study math and science? This is a reasonable option to some of the younger girls because no one has shown them an alternative that is more reasonable. No one has taken the time to prove to them that education is a more steady and reliable path. They see no reason to go to school when they can have everything that they want without their education. The representatives from their environment are having a tremendous impact on their decisions.

It does not seem like an impossible dream when a child from the projects believes that he can grow up and make millions playing basketball, because he looks on the television and sees guys who are just like him and grew up like him. He knows that there are lots of guys in the NBA that have come from the projects and have elevated themselves to another level of society. They walk and talk like them, dress like them, and listen to the same music, so they believe that they can be one in the same.

In my old neighborhood, I didn't know a single person who had gone to college before me. So I had no examples of the benefits of obtaining a higher education. So right or wrong, at the beginning of my teenage years, I never seriously considered going to college because I didn't believe that college was an option for me. I didn't see education playing any role in my quest for success. But at the same time, I did believe deeply in my heart, that one day I would be a professional basketball or a football player. Not necessarily because of any immense talent that I possessed but simply because I regularly saw those examples. Countless athletes from Detroit have gained success on the playing field. Because of the athletes that had gone before me, I also believed that I could be a great athlete. I wasn't aware of any other options to change my circumstances. Because I couldn't see it, it was difficult for me to believe it.

I promise you that you can find plenty of kids from the bleak city streets of Detroit that believe they will one day gain sports fame. Now tell the same kid that he will grow up to be a world leader in corporate finance and watch the look on his face. I am pretty sure it will be a look of disbelief. Not because he doesn't have the talent, but because he has probably never seen it done so it makes it a little more difficult to digest. Allow this same child to be exposed to the proper environment, where there are black success stories and now this image is not so foreign. Introduce this kid to Richard Parsons, the CEO of AOL-Time Warner and no longer does it seem impossible. He realizes that it really is possible when he sees Kenneth I. Chenault, CEO of American Express, or E. Stanley O'Neil, CEO of Merrill Lynch. Collectively, these black men are controlling billions of dollars. Let this young man read Dr. Ben Carson's books and now he realizes that he really can do it.

You must understand that our children believe that they can become what they see, as did I believe that I could become what I saw. Unfortunately, some of our children see a lot of drug dealers that are driving nice cars and have lots of money and some of our children want to pattern themselves after them. They become distracted by the money and the material things and don't count the consequences of living that lifestyle.

The sad thing is that many of our youth do not have the power to control the environment that they were born in. Some have been born to parents that are still very young themselves and have not accumulated the financial means to move them to a safer neighborhood. When you are in the sixth grade, you feel powerless to tell the drug dealers to find another corner to hang out on.

So what options does a child like this have? Although things may seem impossible to overcome at times, there are many things in life that we still have a lot of control over. One thing that we definitely can control is who we allow to be our friends. If you want to be successful then do not associate yourself with people that are not on that same path as you are. Eventually they will just drag you down with them. It can be a difficult thing to do at times but it may be necessary for your survival.

What you expose yourself to and who you surround yourself with is very important to your success. Once I made it a point to educate myself in the realm of finance my associations changed. Not my friends but just the group of people that I discussed and took financial advice from. When I talk of educating myself in the realm of finance, I do not mean making more money. I mean having my money make more money for me. There are plenty of people that make six-figure salaries and are still not wealthy. I know that some people find this difficult to believe but it is so true. You can make tons and tons of money, but if you do not know what to do with it, then you will not become wealthy. You will accumulate lots of nice things but nice things do not equate with wealth. I completely reorganized the circle of people who I discussed these issues with. As a surgeon, it wouldn't make much sense to get a second opinion from an accountant regarding medical issues. It makes no sense at all does it? So don't share your dreams of becoming an entrepreneur with someone that will always pack boxes on the assembly line. They will have no positive input into your situation. Go and find an entrepreneur and share your dreams with them.

I had no choice if I was to truly change my financial position. I was guilty of asking advice from people that really don't have a clue. Why do we ask financial advice from people that are not rich? We do it because it is easy and convenient. In my mind, if you are not wealthy then you are not the person that I need to pattern myself after to accumulate wealth. It is easy to ask my cousin or my friends from college financial questions. It takes more effort to find new associations. It takes more effort to go to the bookstore and pick up titles on subjects that interest me. I'll miss television programs if I go to seminars at night after work or on the weekends. You must be aggressive when it comes to your future. You have to go out and take it, because no one is going to give it to you.

I try to always tell students that if they know someone that is presently doing a type of job that they would like to do themselves later in life, then they should approach that person and ask them to become a mentor for them. If the person says no then move on to the next person doing the same thing. The point is not to get discouraged, and do not give up. If you want to learn something, why take advice from someone who does not even work in that field? Unfortunately, this is what we allow to happen. We ask advice from everyone except the people who are working and living in an area that we find interesting. A bank robber doesn't go looking in trash cans for money, he goes to where the money is, the bank. Stop wasting your time going to the wrong sources for your information.

If the people that you hang around are not talking about moving on to better things and improving their lives, then these are not the people that you need to be around. Your environment is extremely important to your success. You have more control over your environment than you think you have. Do not hang around negative people.

If all of your friends are satisfied with having nothing, then you need a new group of friends. If poverty doesn't anger your friends, then you need a new group of friends. If ignorance does not anger your friends, then you need a new group of friends. If living on public assistance doesn't bother your friends, then you need a new group of friends.

If your friends are not actively making efforts to change their life, then you need a new group of friends. Not just talking about making a change, but actively making change.

You must take control of your mental environment as well as your physical environment. Be cognizant of the types of television programs that you watch and the music that you listen to. Everything in your environment has a contribution, whether positive or negative.

If the people around you walk around with that self-defeating attitude, then you need to stop hanging around those people. If the people around you constantly have that, 'Black people ain't gon' never be nuthin' attitude, then you need to remove yourself from these people.

My approach to success has been to surround myself with people that have more than me and know more than me. We need to dump pride in the garbage and leave it behind, because it can really hinder you. Do not think that you are so good that you cannot humble yourself and ask someone for help. I not only associate with people that have more than me and know more than me, I am the initiator of these interactions. I don't wait for them to speak to me in the hallway, I go up to them. I don't wait for them to call me, I call them. I don't sit by the phone hoping to be invited out for dinner. I set up dinner and invite them out, so I can pick their brain.

Surround yourself with people moving in a positive direction. It is not going to be easy, but it is necessary, if you want greater things out of life. Now, if you are happy where you are, and you are comfortable with where you are, then it is o.k. to keep the friends that you have.

Environment is critical, a planted seed must have proper soil, water, and light. One of the best decisions that I have ever made was to go away for college. It really wasn't that far away when I compare it to some universities in the south or out east. But it was miles away in terms of the mentality and the living conditions.

I attended Michigan State University for my undergraduate education. It is about eighty miles west of Detroit, or an hour and half drive. Some of the lessons that I learned by being in a new environment have proved to be more valuable than the science that I learned while I was a student there.

What did my new environment have that was so different? There was no liquor store on every corner. There were no beer bottles and trash all over the streets. I didn't see any crack houses. I was exposed to an entirely different environment now. I was around kids that were driving $30,000 and $40,000 sports utility vehicles.

My parents never owned a car that expensive. I was invited to Christmas parties at $300,000 homes in the suburbs. I had seen these things on television, but I had never personally experienced it.

I was starting to see that there was a better life to be lived. I started to see that life was much bigger than Detroit. I had never been outside of Detroit for any considerable amount of time until I went to college. I didn't know any parents that bought their kids BMWs.

By growing up in Detroit, I believed all of my past experiences were the normal way of life in America. I had no idea how much better life could really be. Seeing abandoned houses had been the norm for me. In East Lansing I never saw an abandoned building. There was no city wide alert of the armed forces for devil's night violence. Things that were everyday occurrences in Detroit were now repulsive to me. My tolerance level had changed considerably.

While my friends and I flooded the financial aid office, I had many white friends who had never heard of a Stafford Loan. After seeing these things, it motivated me to obtain more and provide for my children in the same manner. I saw an opportunity that I was not going to let slip by. Being in a new environment motivated me tremendously. It showed me that living around poverty didn't have to be a normal occurrence.

I had literally stumbled onto a gold mine. I had stumbled onto the keys that could literally unlock my potential and change my future. I had found what I needed to get out of the ghetto. This discovery was not intentional, by any means. I did not have some grand master plan to become a surgeon and entrepreneur. I went to college because I didn't have anything else to do. I was just tired of sitting around, drinking beer all day, and hanging out all night. But once I was exposed to a new environment, the light bulb in my head went off and I have never looked back. This change may have never occurred if I would have never been willing to change my environment.

At home, in my past environment, I never saw anything to encourage me, or to convince me, that I could have a better life. Once I removed myself, I could see and touch the reality of a better life, and I now believed that it was for me specifically.

Now that I lived in a different environment, the things that were everyday occurrences in Detroit no longer sat well with me. Since murder was not a topic in Okemos Michigan, where my apartment was, news about it from Detroit struck a cord in me more than it had when I lived there. Murder is never acceptable, but when you hear about it every single day of your life, it just doesn't shock you anymore. I was no longer flooded with daily news of drug raids and drive-by shootings. When I was outside of Detroit, and now looking back home with a different view, it hurt me that many of our people will never leave this environment, and may never know that there is more to life. Even worse, I now realized why it is so difficult to make it out of such a rough environment, because if your mind never knows that there is better, you will never reach for better.

That is why it is so critically important to change your environment. You must change it to one that is more conducive to the direction that you are trying to go. You have no idea how many different kinds of people are out there with so many different ideas and connections to help you reach your dream. Even if you don't know where you want to go, you definitely know where you don't want to end up. When I left for college, I never imagined that life could be better than what I was currently living. What I did know was that my life would never get better sitting around drinking beer all day, and working at a toy store tossing boxes for minimum wage. Plant your seeds in a fertile environment and watch them grow.

CHAPTER 11

POSSIBLE CONSEQUENCES

So what will happen if you choose not to become educated? No one can answer that question. There are many possibilities that may occur. The outcome of your life is not etched in stone if you do or do not obtain an education. Obtaining a degree does not promise you a million dollar salary and a private jet. Getting a diploma from a university guarantees you nothing. Even if you never pursue your education, it certainly doesn't mean that your life will be a failure. In my personal experience however, you will miss out on a lot of the things that life has to offer if you are uneducated. The person that makes it big after dropping out of high school is a rare person.

I am not saying that going to school is the only way that you can achieve success and fulfill your dreams, but it will definitely increase your chances of getting where you want to be in life. Getting an education opens more doors, and affords you more opportunities than are granted to those who choose not to become educated. Whenever I mention education, I am not just referring to formal university education. There are many ways to become educated without every stepping foot on a college campus.

Where you end up in life is a choice. The position that you are in today is because of the decisions that you have made in the past. This is true whether or not you consider yourself to be in good position or a bad position. If you feel that you are successful and are happy with where you are, look back over the last few years of your life and think about the decisions that you've made. If you are down on yourself and disappointed in your results, look no further than in the mirror and think about the decisions that you have made over the course of your life. Where you end up in the future is dependent on the decisions that you make today.

There have been many times when I have tried to encourage not only education, but high achievement within education, I have been given the response, "School is not for me." Even if this is true, it should not be an excuse that we use to cover up our laziness. It is true that some of us don't enjoy learning and participating in formal education as much as others, but I think that this should be looked at in its proper context. Before you make this statement I think that there are other things that you should consider. Sure, it would be more understandable to shrug school off if you had a big inheritance waiting for you, or if your dad owned some large corporation which he was grooming you to command someday. Most of us are not in these select groups, so it would be in our best interest to increase our knowledge through education, which in turn will increase our power.

So o.k., school is not for you. Now what are you going to do? Who or what generous bank is going to finance your fabulous business plan? Do you have any collateral to offer? Will you receive an inheritance to start off your life? Does a Fortune 500 company have a corner office reserved for you with stock options, benefits, and a company car? Can you sing like Luther Vandross or play ball like Jordan? After answering these questions I think that you need to reconsider whether or not school is for you. I have met many people making poor wages and living below their potential that felt like school wasn't for them either.

Education is vital, regardless of the career you choose. Remember, when I talk of education, I do not mean specifically a degree from a major university. Think about how many times we have heard the stories of entertainers that have lost their millions. The reason is because they have not educated themselves in the area of finance. Even though they have made the money without becoming educated, they have not been able to keep the money without being educated. We have followed the careers of entertainers of whom performances we know so well, only to find out later that they have not kept even a fraction of the enormous amounts of money that we assumed that they had been paid. The producers and owners of entertainment make even more than the performers we flock to see. The difference between many of the owners and producers of entertainment, when compared with the performers, is that the owners and producers more often than not have a stronger knowledge of the business and the financial matters of the entertainment industry. Because of this greater knowledge they come out better financially in many instances than the performers themselves and we don't even know their names. The owners and producers many times cannot sing a single musical note.

Many of us admire certain entertainers and can recite their songs verbatim. We purchase their albums, concert tickets, and many times we follow them throughout their careers. However, too often, their managers and producers reap the financial benefits of these entertainers' talents. The reason for this is because some entertainers do not take the time to educate themselves in the realm of finances and the negotiation of their contracts. Because of this, many of them come up on the short end of the stick when it comes to money, even though they may have worked so very hard to get the fame that they have obtained. Are you starting to see why knowledge is so important in your life? Having talent is not enough.

Sometimes, even when entertainers are fortunate enough to actually receive what they are worth to the industry, they still die broke because of poor decisions when it comes to money and finance. Many times they put their trust, their money, and their future in the hands and control of another. They can end up getting taken for large sums of money that they have worked so hard for.

The above scenario has played itself out over and over again. The lack of knowledge and the lack of education is the key to our downfall time and time again. Because we don't learn the causes of heart disease and change our lifestyles it remains the number one killer in America. I submit to you a new way of looking at this. Yes, heart disease is the number one cause of death in America, but I believe that the lack of knowledge is the true number one killer in America. I believe that heart disease is the symptom and not the disease itself. The real disease is ignorance. If we learn better eating habits, as well as exercise, and apply them to our life, the incidence of heart disease should decline. The knowledge of how to prevent heart disease is our greatest weapon in this scenario. It always goes back to knowledge.

When I was in college, I worked mostly during my Christmas and summer vacations so that I could obtain extra money for my clothes and other things. I have had many different work experiences. I have solicited surveys over the telephone for soft-drink companies, and I have cut vegetables for the university food system. I have been a janitor mopping up floors and cleaning up other people's urine. My parents couldn't afford the $10,000-a-year I needed to go to undergraduate school so I worked to make extra money, and the remainder of the money that I needed I obtained from school loans, grants, and scholarships.

There is one work experience that I will never forget. This is the one experience that opened my eyes to what my possible future may hold if I did not go back to school and complete my education. I was a sophomore in college at the time and like the previous summer I headed home. My roommate and I had heard from a mutual friend about a good summer job to put some extra money in our pockets. To get this job, we had to apply through a temporary agency. For those of you that do not know what a temp agency is I will explain. Their sole purpose is to interview and place mostly unskilled workers in low paying jobs for some of the large warehouses and factories. After they interview you and determine your level of skill or education, then they find an open position for you wherever the need is. The three of us were all placed in the same warehouse. This warehouse packaged small automobile parts for one of the major automobile companies. We packaged things like headlight bulbs, mufflers, rotors, etc. At first it seemed like a nice little job for the summer before we were to go back to school. I had no idea what it was really like to work in a place like this.

The pay started at $4.50 an hour. We had to get up at 6:00 in the morning to start out our day. We would get a $.25 raise each week if we didn't miss any work days during that week. Even if you had accumulated enough raises to boost your pay up to $5.50 and you happened to miss a day of work, you would be dropped back down to $4.50 per hour. In every area of the warehouse there was an assembly line, which meant non-stop work with almost no bathroom breaks unless it was time for everyone to take a break. It amazed me how an adult has to ask someone if they could go to the bathroom. I was working there in the summertime and the temperatures in that place had to be near 100 degrees. There was no air-conditioning, just multiple fans placed throughout the building. Even through all of this, it still took a couple of months for it all to sink in just how terrible of a situation this really was. I was just a kid, and I was just happy to be able to buy some stuff.

Although the pay was pathetic, I was nineteen or twenty at the time and it was enough to pay for the little things that I needed. The thing that started to bother me was the number of adults that had to put up with such poor financial rewards. Even the permanent hired in workers were only making $7 an hour. Many of these people had children at home. I couldn't imagine how I could pay my bills and feed someone else on $7 per hour. As I looked closer and closer I really started to understand the situation.

Every day when the lunch truck came I purchased some type

of sandwich and chips. At one point, I noticed that so many people were eating bologna sandwiches or peanut butter and jelly day after day. This is fine if it is by choice, but I would later realize that many people had to do this out of necessity. In today's economy, $7 just does not stretch very far and you end up having to cut corners wherever you can. My co-workers were not doing this because they wanted to, but they were doing this because they had to. Many of them had no choice and they had no options. Their lack of skills and education had left them in a dead-end job making very little money.

None of these workers had gone on to college, and I didn't meet anyone that spent any of their spare time doing things that could better their situations. They all fell into one of the possible consequences of not obtaining more knowledge. If they decided to leave this company where could they go? What did they have to offer a potential employer? When my friends and I headed back to college, these people were forced to stay in these pathetic working conditions because they had no way out. They had no way out because all of their previous efforts up to this point in their lives had not produced anything that they could now use to improve their situation. We have to focus our efforts, time, and energy on things that will improve our situation. If you are spending large amounts of your time, energy, money, and efforts on things that will not improve you or your surroundings or your situation, then you are wasting your time and the people who come after you will be no better off than you are because you will have left them nothing that they will be able to build upon.

The people that worked at this warehouse were suffering from one of the possible consequences of not obtaining an education, working in a dead end job. There was no opportunity for rising up through the company, there was no opportunity for a substantial pay raise, and there were no retirement benefits. I promise you that this is not where you want to end up spending your life.

After toiling in places like this what do you think happens to many of our young black men? Just because your pay scale is low and the level of gratification from your place of employment in zero, it still doesn't change your hopes and dreams. If you have dreams of a comfortable home and a nice automobile with a pocket full of money before being hired into a pathetic job, you will probably still have those same desires after working there for some time. That doesn't change, everyone wants a comfortable life.

The fact that these thirsts are not quenched can be extremely motivating. The unfortunate thing is that too many of our young men allow the energy from this motivation to direct them down the path of illegal behaviors. Going into a demeaning job day after day can start to appear like a no win situation after a while. Many of our young men have friends or relatives that are involved in the drug game or some other illegal activity. They become increasingly bombarded with the temptations of large sums of money and the material things that they believe will satisfy their desires. They see other young men their same age living what they think is the good life of easy money, lots of women, and constant parties. They are invited in and encouraged to participate in this lifestyle. For some of our youth, this is not a difficult decision for them to make. Because in their mind what do they have to lose? They have been lead to believe that it is too late to go back to school. (It is never too late. The oldest person in my first year medical school class was fifty-one years old.) They know that their current job cannot provide them with the resources to keep up with the lifestyle promoted on today's music videos. Almost none of these young men have parents that have the funds to support such a lifestyle. As far as many of them are concerned, the drug game is the best move for them if they ever want to have a better life for themselves or their families.

This is a very sad tale that is played out daily all over the country with our young black men. The glitter of the chrome and diamonds is so bright that it blinds their eyes to the harsh reality and makes it impossible for them to see the obvious things that are right in front of them. What many of them don't see and what their mentors neglect to tell them is that almost no drug dealers retire at an old age. They fail to realize that there is no pension plan for thugs. They can't see that 'playas' eventually get played out. The end result today is the same as it has been for many years. Two destinations are waiting for these young men, prison or the cemetery.

After my first two years of college living in the dormitory I moved off campus. I moved into a three-bedroom apartment with two of my friends. One of my friends had a cousin that would come and visit us quite often. He would bring friends with him that my roommate grew up with back in his old neighborhood. After awhile they would come up a few times a month and would even spend days and weeks at a time with us in our apartment. They came up so often that they were regulars at the parties and other people on campus knew them also. My roommate's cousin happened to be a drug dealer and so were the other guys that he had been bringing with him. At the time it wasn't a big deal to me that he sold drugs. I've had cousins that sold drugs, and growing up in Detroit, I've had many people from my neighborhood choose this lifestyle. It was so common in our neighborhood that it didn't even shock us any longer. I can remember that we had a lot of fun with them when they came up to visit back then. They were just one of our friends just like everyone else that we hung out with.

I can remember on countless occasions, he would say things like, "Man you don't know how good you've got it. I should go back to school, man." "I already have my high school diploma, I should go to college." In my mind I'm thinking, "What is he talking about, he's pulling out one-hundred dollar bills and I'm eating hot dogs and noodles for dinner tonight." It seemed like he would say this every time that he came to visit. "Man, you don't know how good you have got it, I should go back to school." I can remember many times when my friends wanted me to go to parties and I refused to go because I needed to study. It seems like I was always studying, because I wanted to get into medical school. He would speak up and say, "Leave Rod alone man, he needs to study, he's going to be a doctor."

Years later I realized that he was right. We really did have it made. We were on the road to building careers for ourselves. We didn't have to fear the police or worry about being pulled over and being caught with drug possession. We didn't have to look over our shoulders everywhere that we went. We didn't have the stress of living the drug game where you can be killed at any moment and there is no one that you really can trust. No one was out to get us or rob us. We were just college kids having fun.

I did not realize it at the time, but I believe that the reason that my roommate's cousin came up to visit us so often is because it was a place of refuge for him. College was stress-free compared to the things that he had to deal with back home. He could come up there with us and just be a college kid with no cares in the world. He blended in well. He could just lie on the couch all day and play video games and just hang out with the rest of the college kids. When he was at college with us, he didn't have to be the leader of a drug operation.

Do not ever forget that you will reap what you sow. The seeds that you plant will one day come to harvest. After coming to visit us for about a year, I no longer called them my roommate's cousin or my roommate's friends. They had become my friends also. They were not bad guys, they were guys that made bad decisions. One Saturday morning, my roommate paged me and he told me that one of these guys had been killed the night before at a night club in Ohio. He was shot seventeen times. Witnesses said that after the two gunmen ran out of bullets, they stood over him and kicked him in the face and then spit on him as he bled to death. About six months later, my roommate's cousin was arrested and received a ten-year prison sentence for selling drugs.

One of the worst things that I see in the emergency rooms of the Detroit hospitals is wasted talent. I have met many people over the years by being around so many patients in the hospitals. Some of these patients have granted me the opportunity to go a little deeper beyond their present condition and afford me the privilege to learn something about their personal lives. I have asked heroin addicts what made them use the first time. I have asked prostitutes what brought them to that point in their life. When you take the time to talk to people, you realize that there is so much more to them than what you can see on the outside.

After speaking to so many of these people, I have found that many of them are very smart, but they have made very bad decisions. They have wasted the skills and talents that God has given them. When we meet these people in their down trodden state, what we are seeing is the manifestation of poor choices coming to pass. The seeds that you plant today will one day come to harvest. Do not waste the talent that God has invested in you. The possible consequences of not obtaining an education can be a devastating one. Education affords you many options that the uneducated will not enjoy. When you wake up one morning and realize that your opportunities are limited, the temptation to involve yourself in other activities becomes stronger and stronger. Give yourself as many options as possible by becoming educated.

CHAPTER 12

Afraid to Fail

"For God hath not given us the Spirit of Fear, but of Power, and of Love, and of a Sound Mind"
                                                                    -The Apostle Paul

Fear is a very interesting emotion. It can affect many different people in many different ways. It moves some, while it may paralyze others. When I was in medical school, we learned that the body has a natural response when confronted with this situation or this emotion called fear. This theory stated that the response to fear is necessary for human survival and continued existence as a species. The term is called the 'Fight or Flight response'.

We all have experienced this situation knowingly or unknowningly, the fight or flight response. If you have walked out into the street not initially recognizing that an oncoming car was moving towards you. If you have ever been walking down the street and an angry looking stray dog started to come your way. If you have been getting out of your car or exiting a building and a stranger startled you. If you think back on these situations try to remember what your bodies' response was to these encounters. You instantly became more alert. Your respiratory rate started to increase. Your heart rate started to increase. The result of the increased heart rate is the delivery of more oxygenated blood to your brain and to your muscles. These muscles are tensed up and contracted in anticipation of either defending the body or fleeing to protect the body from harm. This is all natural and programmed within you to protect you and increase your chances of survival and perpetuation. Your body released a natural hormone to stimulate this action response. This hormone is called adrenaline or (epinephrine).

The natural boost of energy that comes from epinephrine is for your protection. When you are suddenly placed in harmful situations, you must respond appropriately or risk harm. Simply put, 'fight or flight'. You either defend yourself, or you must flee to fight another day. If either is done ineffectively, then you may perish and so may your descendants that would have been born from your lineage. We were taught that this was constantly in effect in the animal world and on a similar scale in the human existence as well.

I believe that fear is one of our greatest obstacles that we must conquer on the journey of success. Fear hampers many peoples' dreams. Because many of us are afraid to fail, we become afraid to try. Many times we are afraid of what others may say or think, so we don't even try. Fear can hamper us to the point of actually crippling us. Fear can be paralyzing at times, literally preventing us from physically moving to higher levels in life.

One the other hand, fear can be the very fuel that keeps someone alive. I think we have all seen those nature specials that focus on the hunters and the hunted in the animal kingdom. They show these long drawn out chase scenes of the wildcat chasing the rabbit or hare. Sometimes they show the lions or tigers hunting for a meal in Africa. These hunted prey literally use the flight part of the 'fight or flight' response on a regular basis. If they do not use it effectively they and their lineage may perish from the face of the earth.

In this instance, fear is almost like a benefit. It can be like a fire to us. Fire is very dangerous when uncontained and uncontrolled. An uncontained and uncontrolled fire can destroy lives and it can destroy property. When allowed, yes allowed, to go unchecked, fire can completely wipe out what previously stood as a testament to greatness. In its wake there are only smoldering ashes of what once was standing tall and proud.

On the other hand, what can become of fire when it is mastered and wielded to your benefit? It can prevent you from freezing on cold winter nights. It can provide light to you as you travel through this wilderness. It allows food to be served to you that is safe to eat, by killing the parasites that would normally infect and harm your body.

Fire or fear can do the same thing for you today. Fear, when used as a motivating factor, can push you to do better and survive in this world. Fear, when properly channeled, can open your eyes and force you to educate yourself. By becoming educated, you will be able to see clearer as you travel. Fire does heat and kill parasites. The fire within you can push you to move so far beyond where you currently are that you will see the benefit of cutting off the parasites around you. The people that mean you no good at all. The people that are dragging you down.

When I was a boy, my mother always teased me about how I handled my money. She found it quite amusing how I held onto my money for very long periods of time. If I received money for my birthday, it was not uncommon for me to still have that same $25 or $50 dollars six months later, completely untouched. She laughed at me because she knew that if I said that I didn't have any money, that actually meant that I didn't have any money that I was willing to spend. It didn't mean that I was completely broke. She found it quite humorous that someone so young was so uptight about keeping money. Most children spend, spend, and then spend some more, not ever being concerned about being able to replenish the money.

Even as a child I kept my money separate. I had what I was willing to use and what I had designated as savings. I would hold on to money for months and even years without spending it. Why did I do this? Fear. Fear was my motivation in this situation. For some reason, even as a child, I have always been afraid of becoming poor.

Although I didn't grow up rich, we weren't poor either. Both of my parents worked at the post office and this obviously produced a two income household. We had everything that we needed and some of the things that we wanted. I still grew up in 'the hood' as it is affectionately called by Black people. Since I grew up in 'the hood', many of my friends did not have both of their parents in the home. I should not say many of my friends, I should say most of my friends did not have a father in the home. It is quite a shame, but I grew up with more friends that didn't have a father than friends that did have a father in the home. It is not hard to understand how quickly middle class becomes lower class when the income has been cut into half of what it was or what it should have been if both parents were contributing.

Because of this, many of my friends and cousins were flat broke and some of them were on welfare. I learned at a very early age that poor people live a very different life when compared to those that are financially stable. Poor peoples' options are very limited. Many live in substandard housing and suffer through horrible conditions. Unfortunately, many times they are not treated with much respect either. This is something that should not have anything to do with the size of their bank accounts. For some reason, people just don't roll out the red carpet and speak highly of you when you whip out a big book of food stamps at the store. When speaking to women on the WIC program, many of them report how badly they are treated when applying for or renewing their funds. It became quickly apparent to me at a young age that I would not let this become my destiny. If you haven't been able to tell by now, I am a big fan of having options. It just appears to me that the lower your education level and the lower your income level, then the fewer options that you have in life and the more bitter the pill is that is forced down your throat. A women being disrespected at the WIC office has what options of retaliation for the offense? Their position makes them feel powerless because they are in fear of losing their assistance.

Because of this I have been afraid to be poor for most of my life. It is a fear that would just eat at me all the time. For this reason, even as a young boy, I would save money for years without touching it. The amounts of monies were very small. But in my small mind, it meant a lot to always be able to put my hands on it if I needed it for an emergency or for whatever reason. I felt that as long as I had some money stashed away somewhere I would never be poor.

When I was initially struggling in college I would mentally challenge myself with all kinds of scenarios. After my freshman year in college my grandmother died. It was the first time in my life that someone that close to me had died. I had never felt that helpless before. That situation really woke me up. After her death, I used to ask myself what would happen to me if both of my parents were killed in an auto accident simultaneously. At nineteen years old how would I support myself? My awakening to the understanding of the fragility of life forced me to become aggressive about securing my financial future. I feared that at any moment, by some tragic event, I could be forced out into the world with no parents to guide me and no financial backup. I realized at this point that no matter how hard college was I had to get the most out of it to put myself into a stronger financial position.

Am I still afraid of becoming poor? No, this is not a fear that bothers me anymore. As I am writing this chapter in 2002 our economy is in a downturn. People are losing their jobs by the tens of thousands. Multimillion dollar corporations are going belly up. You will be glad to know that I don't lose a wink of sleep at night. As a matter of fact, my wife tells me that I snore too loud and I sleep too hard to hear the baby crying.

I already know what some of you may be thinking. Some of you may be assuming that my next statement will be that I am no longer afraid to be poor because I have accumulated wealth. Wrong! I am no longer afraid to be poor because I have accumulated knowledge and understanding. Have you ever heard the phrase, "Give a man a fish and you will feed him for a day, but teach a man to fish and you will feed him for a lifetime."? You are looking at a fisherman today.

If you don't get anything else out of this book, please understand that last statement. Once you learn how to fish, you should never go hungry ever again. What happens though is that when we go to work everyday to punch someone else's clock, someone is giving us fish (paycheck), but we are not the fisherman. By the time they have laid us off it is too late. All of the time that we were in the company we didn't take advantage of the resources available to us to learn how to fish. We were just content with our can of sardines every one or two weeks, depending on the cycle of the paychecks.

I know that some people reading this are going to think that I am no longer afraid to be poor because of the size of my banking account and that I was about to go on to explain what kind of fancy car I drive or how big my house is or what kind of investments I have. Many of us tend to have this wealth thing all mixed up. We see someone in an expensive car and assume that they are rich. Material things are only symbols of wealth and do not represent true financial stability. I am not afraid of being poor because of what is in my head and what I know in my heart.

For as long as I can remember, I have always been a sports fan. When I first started following sports, it wasn't common for an underclassman to leave school early to play pro ball. A common saying that the old people use to say was, "Get your education first. Once you have that they can't take it away from you." I never use to understand what the last part of that statement really meant..."once you have that they can't take it away from you". That statement has become absolutely crystal clear to me today. It means the exact same thing as the fisherman statement. Knowledge and understanding is transferable. Wherever you go, your mind goes as well. As long as you know how to fish, you should never go hungry. A job is a job is a job. When that company finds no use for you any longer you are tossed to the side like yesterdays garbage. If all you know how to do is press widgets and the widget plant closes, then what will you do? When your mind is strapped with ammo, then who cares if the plant closes? If the hospital that I work at folded, my life would continue on. I am not tied to a hospital. The knowledge of how to operate is not in the hospital, it is in my head.

We must conquer this fear of failing. It can be paralyzing at times. If a baby is ever to learn to walk, he is going to fall down many many times in the process. On your road to success, you are going to stumble at times. We all know that Donald Trump is very wealthy. Take note of the fact that he has also lost millions before. These are only temporary setbacks. We make them permanent setbacks when we refuse to get up and keep going. Focus on your failures only long enough to learn from them. Hank Aaron is the 'home run king'. He has hit the baseball out of the park more times than anyone in the history of baseball. Even more times than the famed Babe Ruth. What you really need to understand is that he had hundreds of strikeouts to go along with all of those home runs. If he had stopped trying because of all of his misses (failures), he would have never become the greatest home-run hitter of all time. The same is true for you today. If you stop because of the fear from your past failures, you will never become the great achieving person that you could have been.

Don't let fear paralyze you. Get up and move forward. Let's take a moment and look at the life of a paraplegic. This is a person that has no motor or sensory function from the waist down. Their leg muscles don't work and they don't feel any pain or any other sensation from the waist down. We see these people and we feel compassion for them instantly. We see how things like shopping are a struggle for them. We see how difficult it is for them to get in and out of buildings. We see how people abuse their designated handicapped parking spaces, even though they have full use of their limbs.

We see all of these things and we feel sorry for the paralyzed person. Most of us only know of their outward problems that we just discussed. Most of us don't know deep down how difficult their lives have really become. Far beyond the parking spaces and the grocery store shelves.

Many of you may not be aware that since the spinal cord is dysfunctional, many of these people do not know when they need to use the restroom because the sensation that you feel when it is time to go they no longer possess. Because of this, every so often, they must use a catheter to empty their bladder, which increases their chances for a bladder infection. Every so often, many of them have to use a gloved hand to manually remove the stool from their rectum. They have no sensation that tells them that it is time to go. If they are unfortunate enough to contract diarrhea, they don't realize it until they have already soiled their pants and they start to smell their stool.

Since they have no feeling below the waist, they don't sense pain. Either themselves or their caretakers need to move them every two hours to prevent pressure sores from developing. When you sit in a chair for too long your butt starts to hurt. Unconsciously you shift and move your weight all day long to relieve the pressure on your buttocks. This prevents you from developing pressure sores on your bottom. Paraplegics don't feel this pain once they become paralyzed. They can sit there for hours without it bothering them. So a sore is no big deal if you can't feel it right? Wrong. These sores cause the skin to break down. After the skin breaks down then the muscle becomes exposed and then the bone is exposed. Left untreated, these sores can eventually become infected, which can lead to sepsis, amputations, or even death. All stemming from being in one place for too long.

As you can see, paralysis goes much deeper than what we see on the surface. How much longer are you just going to sit there, paralyzed by fear? Unable to move. Have you been sitting there so long that you don't even feel the pain of your situation? Many of our black comedians make jokes about the ghetto and the food stamps and the welfare lines. We just soak it up and laugh and laugh and laugh. At some point you have to become serious about your future. They can afford to make jokes about it because they are no longer using food stamps. Some of us are actually on public assistance and consider this a humorous thing. I can never believe that being poor is funny. Some of us have become so numb to our surroundings that it doesn't even bother us any more.

To be honest with you, when it comes to challenges to my success, I have taken this fear thing to a whole different arena. As a child I used it as a motivating factor. Now I've gotten to the point where it is no longer even in the equation. I keep myself motivated by the fact that "FAILURE IS NOT AN OPTION" for me.

Before I explain to you how I came about using this statement let's just go over a few things for a moment so that I can get you up to speed. This is how medical education works. First, a four year degree is required before entrance into medical school is possible. After completion of medical school, most students around the country have accumulated a similar general fund of knowledge. When each student has decided what kind of doctor they want to be it is then time to branch out into their different fields of choice. The people that want to take care of children go into pediatrics, and the people that like action go into emergency medicine, while the people that like surgery obviously go into surgery and so on and so on. However, this is not as simple and cut and dry as it sounds. There are not enough positions available for every person that wants to be a neurosurgeon or a urologist. There are approximately 17,000 United States medical school graduates each year and less than 200 first year positions available in neurosurgery training. So as you can see, competition can become stiff for certain specialties, depending on the number of positions available compared to the number of people applying for them.

I was interested in orthopaedic surgery. This specialty treats diseases of the bones and joints as well as various athletic injuries. While attending a medical conference in New Orleans, I met two emergency room physicians from Detroit. Both of them were black. I asked them for some advice about how to get into my field of choice, orthopaedic surgery. I was hoping to get some insight about making the transition from medical school into the very intense world of residency training. I wanted a few pointers on the application process or some interview tips. You know, some basic do's and don'ts about the whole process.

I am almost embarrassed to share with you what they told me. They both said that I should give it up and choose another specialty because there was no way that a black man was going to get into orthopaedics. Of course I was shocked to hear what I heard. Before we go further let me share some numbers with you.

African Americans make up roughly 12% of the population in the United States. African-American physicians make up just below 6% of the United States physician workforce. That's not even on par with our representative population in this country overall. In the field of orthopaedic surgery specifically, African Americans make up roughly 3% of the physician workforce in the study of orthopaedic surgery.

I understand that it may be uncommon. But uncommon does not mean impossible. Here I am looking up to these guys and just knowing that I am about to receive encouragement and a wealth of information, and the only thing that they could tell me was to give up and switch to another specialty. I don't know why I said what I said or where it came from, but my immediate response was, "failure is not an option." I said it with confidence and I believed it. They both chuckled in disbelief. I told them that I would see them both at the next year's meeting and I would show them that I had been accepted.

I have never seen those two doctors again but from that day forward I have lived by that statement. When I enter into an endeavor, I literally remove failure as a possible consequence. I do not allow it to enter into the equation. Why? Because every action begins with a thought. There is ALWAYS a way. If you don't have the answer, then someone else does. We are very quick to say that something cannot be done without exhausting every last one of our options. Failure really is not an option to me. If I really want to do it, I believe that I can do it.

Think about a car that you like. When you go to purchase a

car, you look inside of them and you browse the brochure looking at all the possible options. If you ask the sales person for something that is not offered on the car then you remove it from the possible scenarios. No matter how good of a negotiator you may be, you cannot get an option that is not available. As a matter of fact, eventually the salesperson is going to look at you strangely if you continue to ask for something that is not available. Kind of like the strange look I give to people when they tell me that I am going to fail at something. All the while, knowing that failure is not an option that is offered on this vehicle. You can ask to speak with the manager if you want, it will do you no good. The option that you want to have on your car is not one of the possible choices. No matter how much you doubt me, failure is not offered as one of my possible outcomes. Remove failure from your list of possible outcomes. Make failure something that is not even associated with what you are trying to do. Remove the idea of failure from your mind. It is not an option. Don't be discouraged by what others may say to you, because people are going to doubt you. Accept it and move on. Unfortunately many people judge what you can do by what they believe they can do. These two doctors had doubts about what they could accomplish, so there was no way that I could do any better. Right? Wrong! Today, I am Dr. Roderick Claybrooks, Orthopaedic Surgeon. Who do you want to be?

Whoever you want to be, you must overcome any fears that are holding you back. Stop worrying about what people may say about you. Stop worrying about 'what if I don't make it'. Stop worrying about looking stupid. You cannot sit back and let your life pass you by because you are afraid to try. There are too many things out here for you to enjoy to allow fear to keep robbing you of your destiny.

CHAPTER 13

How to Choose a College and a Career

How do you go about choosing the right college for you? Although it may seem like a simple decision, if not thought out and properly considered it could prove to be a grave mistake later on. First, let me tell you that there is no perfect college nor is there a perfect method for choosing one. I do believe that by going about your selection process in a very careful manner it may decrease the headaches later on.

Let me first tell you how I chose my college. Be sure to take note of the faults in the way that I chose my school. I am from

Detroit Michigan and I wanted attend a school that was not far from my home, as many kids decide to do. My first and only choice was Michigan State University. This school was not too close and it was not too far, the distance was just right for me. I didn't choose this school because of its academic reputation or because I had a relative that was an alumnus of the school. I chose it because of its large student population, and because it was known as a party school.

FAULT #1. You should choose a school because of how it benefits you, and gets you closer to your ultimate goal (which should be excelling in the career of your choice). It should not be based on whether or not you will be taught to drink a twelve-pack without stumbling. In my case, MSU turned out to be an excellent choice, and I was very well prepared for the next level. I am thankful that in spite of my poor reasoning I ended up at a school that in fact does have very strong academics.

Schools that have big time academic reputations are sometimes all hype, and the education turns out to be no better than one you can receive at a less well known university. In my part of the country, there is a well-known school that has an excellent reputation among other universities, and whose academics are supposed to be superior to other universities in this part of the country. I didn't find this to be the case. My medical-school class was made up of about 55% graduates from this particular school, and I was neither impressed nor astounded one bit by their supposed superior education. They did not appear to be any smarter or more prepared than anyone else in the class.

One thing that I did notice as I passed through medical school was that the reputation from these big name institutions garnered you a lot more respect, regardless of if it is deserved or not. Students from these big-name programs were immediately recognized, and it was assumed that they knew what they were talking about. This may not seem like much to those of you who have not ventured out on the interview trail, but sometimes a name alone will get your foot in the door. If you are from a well-respected university, you get more interviews, better chances of obtaining the job of your choice, more leverage, and more contacts to use later on (because a lot of time it is not what you know but who you know) .

In general, it opens more doors for you. Let me give you a hypothetical situation. Let's say I graduated from Harvard with just-average grades and I was competing with another student with excellent grades from the University of Kool-Aid. As a graduate from Harvard with just-average grades, I would be very seriously considered for the job for several reasons. First, Harvard has a rep-utation of being one of the finest universities in the world, therefore the assumption is that any product that they produce is coming from such an outstanding pool of students that the candidate is still very good, even if they rank low among the students at Harvard. Second, being average in a pool of the top high school students in the country is nothing to scoff at. It is like looking at an average pro-fessional athlete who rides the bench. When competing against the hall of fame players he or she may not look impressive. But to even be chosen to play at that level you have to be very good, regardless of your performance at that level. If you were at your local park play-ing pick-up basketball, I guarantee that you would choose the twelfth man from any NBA franchise to be on your team before you would pick someone from your neighborhood. Third, coming from a more powerful university increases the chances that someone who wrote you a letter of recommendation will be well known or even personally known by the person interviewing you. Again, it is not always what you know but who you know.

Even though the honor student from the University of Kool-Aid had outstanding grades, some will say that his credentials were built against inferior competition. Neither one of these hypothetical situations are concrete or etched in stone, but they are definitely things to keep in mind. You can excel and go on to a successful career coming from both types of universities.

Ultimately the decision should be yours. I recommend con-sidering the following when choosing a college or university.

1) **The school's ability to fulfill your goals.** This is the number one priority because this is the main reason that you are making the sacrifice of going to school. If you want to become a doctor, do not go to a university that has placed one student in medical school in the last ten years. Some schools have a reputation for certain types of graduates going into certain fields. For example, the Ivy-league schools brag about how many presidents they have produced. If you are interested in a particular school, give them a call and request their information (there is no fee for this and they'll be happy to send it to you). It will describe everything about the school and will definitely boast their strong points. Remember, these schools make money from your tuition, so they will be very eager to sell you their product.

2) **Comfort.** You cannot concentrate and think straight when you are uncomfortable. If you are from Miami or California and cold weather makes you depressed, maybe coming to school in Michigan is not the best decision for you. If being too far away or too close to your parents and siblings will be a distraction, then some lengthy thinking about location should come into play. If being the only black or minority student in a classroom (a very real possibility) is a problem, then find out about the minority population at your school. WARNING; if this is a problem for you then you will eventually have to learn to deal with it. I am from Detroit where almost everyone is black. What I quickly realized is that the world outside of my small world is not like that. You need to understand that this planet is moving closer to Globalization where we will be dealing with any and every type of individual on the planet. If you only know how to relate to blacks, you will be in trouble and will be left behind. Depending on your career, there may be very few blacks working with you (look back at the statistics for orthopaedic surgery). Do not let prejudice, whether internal or external, stop you from getting what you deserve for yourself or your family. You need to be able to work along side everyone.

Comfort does not only involve the above things mentioned. Comfort is everything that you require to set you at ease. Talk to people who have attended certain universities and see what types of students go there. Having like-minded friends is a definite bonus. Also having friends from your part of the country may give you someone to relate to while in a strange area.

Make sure you find out about the surrounding communities also. This will give you an idea about how you will be able to spend your free time when all the studying is done. Is the university the only thing that makes up the city, and once you leave the campus you find yourself in the desert? Or, is the university in the middle of a thriving city? Either of these scenarios may be appealing to different groups. Those of us who are seeking refuge from the hustle and bustle of the city may seek a secluded school where they can hear themselves think. Some prefer the city atmosphere because it provides access to more entertainment. Try to find out what some of the student-body does in their free time. Many universities offer tours of their campus.

3) **Parents preference.** Sometimes this can be a very difficult situation. Especially when the parents are paying for the education. Sometimes parents encourage their children to attend certain schools because that's where they attended or it's the school that they always dreamed of attending. What the student has to remember is that they will be the one taking the exams and going to class. They will be the one up at 2:00 a.m. the night before the final exam while their parents are at home sleeping well. This is why the school has to be a place where the student wants to be. It is very difficult to thrive in a place that you do not want to be. Although sometimes an impossible argument for the student to win, it doesn't hurt to just talk to your parents about it before making a decision that you will have to live with for the rest of your life. All of us want to please our parents, but when pleasing our parents means less than optimal results for ourselves, then this is something we must think long and hard about. Realize that by the time most of us are making these college and career choices our parents have already lived approximately two-thirds of their lives already. Although some may try, it is impossible for them to relive their lives through us. I admire and

respect anyone who can put their dreams and aspirations on hold for a loved one. We must be mindful of the fact that our parents have sacrificed much for us to even be at this point in our lives. My advice to you is to pray long and hard about your decision and weigh all of your options.

4) **Finances.** This should be the least of your worries. In all the years of my education, I personally only knew one black student whose entire education, including housing and living expenses, was completely paid for by his parents. All the rest of my friends, including myself, were either on loans, scholarships, or both. Financial Aid is available from your own United States government, by the way of loans and scholarships. DO NOT BE AFRAID TO GO INTO DEBT TO GET WHERE YOU WANT TO BE. I believe that this is one of our major obstacles. Since we do not have money, we assume that we cannot go to school. I took out nearly $100,000 in loans to obtain my education. People used to tell me that there was no way that they could have gone to school for so long and paid so much money to go to school. My response is always the same, "What else would I have done in the meantime? Would I have been able to just relax on the beach in Mexico?" Not!

Where would I have gotten the money to do that? If I hadn't gone to school, I would have accepted a low-paying job that provided no opportunity for advancement or higher wages. By the time I would have reached twenty-seven years of age (the age that I became a doctor), I would have been no better off and definitely no further in life. So why not take out some loans to go to school? It's better than just sitting at home and doing nothing with your life.

While in high school, I started working odd jobs until I graduated. Sometimes I worked as much as 32-36 hours a week. While in college, I worked during every summer vacation except for one. I took one summer off to study for my medical school entrance exam.

Anything worth having is worth working for. So if you have to work and go to school at the same time, then do it. Do what you have to do to get the money for school. Do not let the lack of finances be your hindrance. As cruel as it may sound, a lot of times the people who do not go to school end up working for the people who did go to school.

FAULT #2. I did not financially prepare myself for college. I was not the type of person that was groomed or raised to be a college graduate. There was no one in my family that had gone to college, therefore there was no one that had experienced the financial challenges of college that could give me a warning. Had I known all along throughout my youth that I would be attending a major university then I could have prepared myself better. So as a child, how do you get financially prepared to spend over one-hundred thousand dollars? By expecting to go to school for free. How do you go to school for free someone is asking? Well you do it by having someone else pay for it. I do not mean a rich uncle when I say this (but if you have a rich uncle then take full advantage), I mean scholarships. Every year, hundreds of thousands of dollars are given away to all different types of students with all different types of backgrounds.

Every single scholarship out there is not just for the person with the 4.0 GPA. There are so many scholarships available for certain ethnic groups, certain genders, for people with certain career goals, we just have to look for them. Most libraries can assist you with sources of potential funds for college. Many authors have devoted entire subjects on how to get funding for college, but we have to be willing to look long and hard to find these books.

Even if we find that we do not fit into one of these categories to obtain money for school, there is always the way of the star student. These kids have the super GPA's and are in the honor societies. To me, this seems like the best way to get a free education. Thousands of these kids get free rides to college every year. Let's stop believing that this path is always for someone else. Let's start to believe that this path is for us. You can be a star student and you can achieve greatness. There is no question in my mind that you have the potential in you to go to school for free.

FAULT #3. The third mistake I made was assuming that the predominantly black colleges and universities like Howard, Morehouse, and Hampton, to name a few, were not good places for me. PAY ATTENTION. My reasoning was flawed and described as follows. I assumed that since the world was financially dominated by whites, going to a predominantly black school would not equip me to handle this type of environment in the workplace. I assumed that I would be lulled into this fairytale world were everyone was black and beautiful, only to be thrust out into a world I wasn't prepared for. I also made the assumption that I would have a very hard time getting jobs or being accepted for graduate training because of racism and bias. **I WAS WRONG!!!** Do not make the mistake I made. I made my decision without talking to anyone with knowledge of these institutions. In my education and career travels, I have been delightfully surprised to find that graduates of these universities are well accepted and they do very well in the work environment. This has taught me some very important lessons. It taught me that although there is racism in this country, if you can perform at a high level, and are willing to work, there is a job for you, no matter what your color. I do not want you to be lulled into thinking that there will be no opposition, but I want you to know that **there will be opposition,** and I want you to be prepared for it. How do you prepare for it? By being the best or one of the best. If you are either of these, it is very hard to justify not hiring you for the job. But if you are average, then you have no ground to stand on. If you think that these universities are the best places for you, then go for it.

Just think about sports for a moment. It is hard to tell by looking at the television today, but many sports didn't allow blacks to participate many years ago, due to racism. Many of our athletes' talents are so tremendous that only a fool would not hire them to give their team a chance to win. Sports like boxing and horse racing actually removed blacks at one time because they were too dominant. If you become as good as I know that you can be, there isn't anything or anyone in this world that can stop you.

Every friend of mine that has gone to a predominantly black institution has loved it. I have heard comments like, "It was the best decision of my life, there is nothing like it." To be honest with you, I have yet to meet one graduate from one of these universities that has regretted their decision. They all speak very fondly of the times that they had back in college. This may very well be the ideal place for you also. Visit the campus and have a look around and speak to the current students to get a better idea of what it is like.

Now let's get to the business of deciding what kind of career we will have for the rest of our lives. To me, this should be very straightforward, but all too often I talk to people who are not pleased with their current employment. In my opinion, the best way to determine what type of career you would like is to first decide what types of things you like to do most. I came to the conclusion that being a physician was the best career for me based on the fact that throughout high school the only time I was very interested in what was going on in class was when we talked about things that concerned the human body. I enjoyed classes like biology and physiology. Any class that would teach me about the most fascinating creation of all time, the human body, would command my attention. There was little doubt in my mind upon arriving on the college campus that wearing blue suits and sitting in board meetings was not for me. I had to be working with the human body in some way, shape, or form.

The path to your career choice may not be as easy as mine, but don't get discouraged along the way. Do you like to debate and argue? Then maybe being a lawyer is for you. Do you like to deal with capitalism and finances? Then perhaps accounting or financial services is for you. Choose your career based on who you are as a person. This allows the work to flow naturally through you. You do not have to pretend to like what you are doing. I enjoy surgery so much that when I am in the operating room it doesn't even feel like a job to me. I never have a hard time getting out of the bed in the morning when I know that I have to perform operations that day.

Whatever you choose as a career, own it and control it. Do not take all your God-given talents and use them to make someone else rich. When you graduate, work as long as you need to in a company, but always have in the back of your mind that this is a temporary situation, and one day you will be your own boss planting seeds into your own future harvest.

CHAPTER 14

OUR OBLIGATION

"To Whom Much is Given Much is Required"

-Jesus the Christ

Have you ever owed anyone anything? The answer is probably yes. If you are like me, then you have and still probably are in this situation. Once again, if you are like me, it bothers you to be in this position of debt, and it eats away at you, and makes you want to rectify the situation, and pay back what has been given to you. We as a people are in a great deal of debt. I know some of you are saying, "What does he mean? I don't owe anyone anything." But you do and so do I. We are in debt to everyone that has come before us, and we owe something to those who are coming after us.

First and foremost I owe all of my success and blessings to God. Only through his grace and mercy have I made it to this point in my life, especially since I've done my share of stupid things to inhibit my own progress.

At the same time, for me to even be in the position that I am in, many people suffered for the rights that we so casually take for granted. Just over forty years ago, we couldn't even drink out of the same water fountains that white people drank from, and we had to use certain restrooms that were designated 'for blacks only'.

So the thought of going to medical school had to be extremely hard to imagine for someone who couldn't even sit down and eat anywhere that they wanted to. So why do we owe these people? We owe these people because they refused to accept these types of conditions. By taking a stand and demanding better treatment, they risked their jobs, their health, and even their lives. They marched, they protested, and they refused to give up. Higher education is something that can only be partaken of after the basic necessities of life have been acquired. The last thing on someone's mind is physics problems when they've been told to sit at the back of a bus that their taxes helped pay for. These people fought to obtain the basic things we take for granted everyday. In many instances the people who were part of the 1960's civil rights movement were attacked and treated as less than animals.

I would like for you to close your eyes for a moment. Now imagine it is a scorching July afternoon, and you are walking downtown looking in the store windows at the items on sale. Your shirt is wet with sweat, and the sales paper is not doing you justice as you use it as a fan. You see a water fountain about twenty feet ahead of you right outside of a store. The people at the fountain are staying for seconds and thirds because the water is so cold and good. As you approach the fountain a few people in the line look at you funny but you think nothing of it. You check your shirt for stains, and then you make sure your zipper is closed on your pants. You patiently wait your turn to enjoy the cool liquid. The line moves along and it is finally your turn. As you bend over to drink some water someone grabs your arm and jerks you to get your attention. You look up and it is an officer of the law, and he asks you the strangest question, "Can't you read, nigger?" Before you can answer him, he uses his Billy club to point to a sign that is posted over the water fountain that reads **FOR WHITES ONLY**. Could you imagine this happening to you? Because I can't even begin to understand what it would feel like. Those who came before us had to endure situations like this and much worse.

Sometimes silence tells more about a situation than words. Both of my parents grew up in the south. My father was born in Tennessee, and my mother was born in Alabama. They never ever bring up the fifties and sixties--not ever. We seem not to have problems sparking conversations about the seventies and eighties. When it comes to times surrounding the civil rights movement, most people who lived it don't bring it up. It seems that these times were just too painful to continually relive over and over. My parents never bring it up.

One of the things that amazes me the most when I see the video tapes of the 1960's is the number of older or elderly individuals who were marching and picketing. They were willing to fight a fight where they could literally lose everything they had, including their life, in a battle that no one knew how long would last. They were fighting for rights that many of them would never even get to enjoy.

That is the type of dedication that it takes to become a winner. It takes sacrifice. These people were sacrificing for me, and they were sacrificing for you. This is why I feel indebted to them. Many of those middle-aged and older people knew that they would never benefit from desegregating the schools, but they wanted to preserve something for the next generation. Many of these older people knew that they would never be going off to college, but they wanted the opportunity to be there for anyone who would like to go to college. Their fight and struggle paved the way and opened up many doors that have allowed many people today to obtain success. So to these people I feel a great deal of indebtedness. I believe that one way to repay them is to take full advantage of the rights and the privileges that they made possible for you and I to enjoy. They made it better for the generations coming after them, and I believe that I should do my part to do the same. In some way make things a little better for those coming after me.

Hopefully I can show other children from the city that it is possible for them to be successful. No matter where you were born, and no matter how little you start off with, you can be successful. No one in my family is a doctor, but I did not let that stop me from becoming one. No one in my neighborhood was paving the way to college, but I went anyway.

I challenge you to do the same. I challenge you to make things better for the next generation. Whether or not you can see it, someone has made things better for you. I especially challenge the parents. Our children see us everyday and we should be the greatest influence in their lives.

Unfortunately, it appears to me that many parents have not passed on or stressed the importance of education to our children. We can pass on a new realm of experiences to our children the way that the previous generation left us the possibility to experience freedom on a greater scale than they did. Education can provide a lot of freedom that is just not allotted to the uneducated. It provides new financial opportunities and gives you more control of your life.

We can have a generation of children that have education ranked at a higher level of importance over video games and becoming athletes and entertainers. Not because these are bad things, but because I am a man that believes in taking advantage of opportunity. In the society that we live in, and from my personal experiences, education gives you a better chance of gaining success in life and it affords you more opportunity. That statement is for those of us that weren't born into wealthy families or situations where all we have to do is grow up and our grandfather has a job in the company waiting for us. I have not met many blacks living in this type of situation. Some of us will have to climb from low-middle class or lower, and there are few established opportunities already waiting for us.

So what will you leave your children? What will you leave to the children that are not yours? How many times have we put our own selfish interests and laziness ahead of something that may benefit our children's education? We complain about the school systems, but when was the last time we went to a parent teacher's conference? My teacher-friends tell me that out of a class of 35-40 students, less than ten parents show up for these conferences. It is so ironic that no one shows up but everyone has a problem with the system. Change only comes from action and as long as the people don't act, there will be no change, and the children will suffer and be forced out into a world that they are not equipped to excel in.

For some people, the reality of the world slapping them in the face on a daily basis is too much to handle. Some of our youth see no alternatives to fulfilling their dreams except through a life of crime or dating and socializing with those that participate in crime. If a young man is given an alternative to selling drugs, I believe he will take it. The key is that he must see someone that looks like him that has benefited from the alternative. As long as it is just talk with no action or manifestation, he will never subscribe to it.

Education will not become important to our children until it becomes important to us. A lot of parents don't understand the importance because their parents didn't understand the importance and their parents didn't understand the importance, and so on and so on. We must break this cycle of ignorance. You have to remember, lots of times children become what they see, and not what we tell them they should be. When I was younger, I used to hear adults say, "Do what I say, not what I do." Translation; "I'm irresponsible and I have not gained control over myself, and my actions, even though I know what I am doing is wrong." The end result is that whether the adult was talking about smoking or drinking, is a child that is more likely to grow up smoking and drinking. There is a good likelihood for them to progress to this because this is what they grew up seeing.

So what do our children see us doing? We cannot let our children see us doing nothing, and expect them to be active. Our children won't be excited about learning if we are not excited about it. What do your children see you get excited about? How are you showing your children to plan for their future? Do we teach them to just handle the future when it comes or do we teach them to be active participants in controlling their destiny? Do you teach them that they can improve their situation by standing in the lottery line? Okay, I won't go there, but I think that you get the point.

My point is that every parent has an obligation to their children to guide them in the proper direction. We have an obligation to leave things better for the next generation than they were left for us.

Our focus should be to leave a legacy. A legacy allows things to carry on in our absence. Our children have to be left something to build upon. I hate to say it, but how often are blacks left an inheritance in this country? Many times, we are left nothing but debt. Too many times have I seen someone die and the family has to ante up to pay for the funeral. This just doesn't seem right to me. You live fifty or sixty years and you haven't even accumulated enough to bury yourself? There is something wrong with this picture. A farmer that eats all of his seeds is bound to starve eventually. Not only will the farmer starve, but his children will inherit a barren land with absolutely no tools to cultivate it. So the children start off in no better a position than the parents. This is not progress, this is going in reverse.

Each successive generation should advance more than the last. It becomes very difficult to do this if each successive group starts off at the same position as the last group. Imagine watching a relay race at a track and field meeting. The strange thing is that each time a runner passes the baton the next runner goes back to the starting point. How successful do you think this relay team will be when they are compared to a relay team that passes the baton after making progress and giving the next generation a head start?

We owe it to the generations coming after us to give them a head start in the race. Let's meet our obligations to those that came before us and to those that are coming after us.

CHAPTER 15

To The Parents

Success is a team sport. I do not believe that I can stress to you enough how vitally important parents are to a child's success. Without the parents input, their motivation, and their concern for the outcome, it will be extremely difficult for a child to become an academic powerhouse. Parents must become involved in order for it to work. Academic success does not occur with a hands off approach from the parents. Don't look at school as just a daycare so that you can get a 'break'. Look at school as a time for seeds to be planted into your child's fertile mind. I am also a parent, and I understand how much pressure it can be to work full time, try to pay all of the bills, and still have time for the children. It is so vitally important that you have to find a way to be active in their lives no matter how busy you become with all of the other things that life throws at you. You can't send your children off to school and just assume that everything is fine and put their future on cruise control. If you do they may be cruising right down to the local burger place to sell fries as a career.

I can remember one time when I was listening to a talk radio show and the topic was "The Failing Detroit Public School system". There were many callers calling in and much dialogue going on between the guest and the talk show host. Some people were blaming the Mayor, some people were blaming the city counsel, and some people were blaming the teachers. There were even others that were blaming the children themselves. The guest made a statement that stuck with me for a very long time. What he said was very simplistic and straight to the point, but at the same time it was so profound. His point was that in communities that had been rated as having a good school system, and the children were excelling in academics, there was one thing in particular that these areas had in common. The thing that they all had in common was very high rates of parent involvement in the school system. In areas where the school system is considered to be poor, a lot of times there is very little parent participation, except complaining.

I have many friends that are teachers and they've told me some horrific stories. They feel that they have no support at all when it comes to educating our children. They are being forced to teach in class sizes that are too large, and some of the children do not come prepared to learn, and some don't even want to learn. In order for the children to have materials that are worth anything, some of the teachers have had to use money out of their own pockets to purchase them. Not only that, the salaries that the teachers are paid are quite pathetic in my opinion. Especially when we consider how difficult of a job it is that they must do. We trust them with something that is so vital and so valuable, yet we don't compensate them adequately.

Sometimes the only interaction that teachers have with the parents is when they show up to the school to call themselves 'telling the teacher off' because their child is not doing well in school. In many instances, some parents become very argumentative with the teacher because the child has failing grades or because the child has been disciplined for some type of inappropriate behavior. If the parents were involved from the beginning then it may have been possible to intercept the unproductive pattern that led to the final result of the failing grades. I have been told that these same parents that have so much of a problem with the system are the same ones that are never present at the parent teacher conferences and never participate in school functions. I have one friend who told me that she has had classes of more than 30 students and usually less than 10 parents show up for the parent-teacher conferences. I am not a genius, but I do know that if you put nothing in you will get nothing out.

A lot of times as parents we can become very comfortable with the school system educating our children, and it is not until we see less than satisfactory results do we make an attempt to become involved. A lot of times at this point it still is not really involvement as much as it is complaints and criticism.

These instances of 'telling the teacher off' are very bizarre to me. On one hand, parents send their children off to a system that they obviously are trusting with their child's future, but on the other hand, are very quick to be combative against it. When questioning my teacher-friends, one of their major complaints is that they feel like they do not have any support from the parents. They feel like the parents just drop off the children at the steps of the school and pull off. Many children show up without any supplies to do any school work at all. Some have not even eaten breakfast before school.

When I was a child, parents supported whatever action that was deemed necessary by the teachers and other staff. If you brought home an 'F' then that student was disciplined by the parents. The parents did not go to the school and have a fist fight with the teacher. This is ridiculous! What kind of attitude does that show the child when the parents are arguing, and in some instances having physical confrontations with teachers. As parents we must be very careful about what we allow our children to see us doing.

I have even been told that some parents complain that their child is getting too much homework. Someone please explain to me what too much homework is. Please explain to me how exercising a child's brain, one of his greatest assets, can be a bad thing. But this is the type of destructive mentality that some of us are injecting into our children. What kind of work ethic is a child expected to develop when they see their parents complain on their behalf that the child is been worked too hard or that the child has been disciplined for inappropriate behavior?

I know it can become very difficult to find extra time to be involved in things like education, but it is a must if our children are going to go on to the next level. If we do not find time to become involved in our children's education, then they will have plenty of time to work minimum wage jobs with no benefits. If we do not find the time, it will give them plenty of time to walk down the same paths as so many before them have done. They will join the ranks of the many thousands of other young blacks that never took advantage of the limitless talents that God has invested in them.

One of the problems is that we see activities like this as extra work as opposed to it being a routine part of our lives. It is very easy to fall into the mold of thinking that everything that is necessary for your child's education will be handled at the school and "That's what they are there for," "That's what they get paid to do," "I'm tired when I get off of work," "I don't have any extra time, "I'm working overtime just so he can have clothes on his back." It is very easy and very comfortable to hand over all responsibility to someone else. The truth of the matter is that you have time for whatever you choose to have time for. If it is important enough to you, I guarantee that you will find a way become involved. As long as it is someone else's fault and responsibility, then you'll never have any time.

We all find time to rent movies or go to the cinema. We all find time to watch a few television programs each week. We all find time to have meaningless conversations on the telephone, even though most of these conversations are not geared toward building ourselves up nor making our situation better. We find time to be with our mate for physical pleasure. Some of us find time to go the malls and spend money that we should be investing. Many of us with children find time to go out to clubs. We find time for all of the above things, no matter how many jobs or hours we are working. We find time for all these things no matter how tired we are. We find time for these things because they are important to us. Education will not become important to our children until it becomes important to their parents.

There is a segment of the population that would like to become involved in their children's education but may feel intimidated because they were never successful academically. Please do not allow this trick to plague your spirit. Many of us feel, "Well I was never able to complete high school, so how can I tell him to get better grades and go to college?" There are many different angles to attack this from. The first thing is to remind them that there are better careers out there that you were eliminated from because you did not obtain an education. Be sure to let them know that they don't have to miss out on them if they choose not to. Remind them that there is a better life than the one you may have been able to provide for them. The only parent that needs to be ashamed is the parent that knows that they did not do the best that they could have done. Please do not take the approach of, "I did fine without ever going to school, so can you." Times have changed and the new world is moving at a rapid rate. The old days of graduating from high school and finding a well-paying secure job at the factory are over. If you are depending on some factory or company to take care of you for the duration of your life, you are living a dream. Those days are over. Ask the hundreds of thousands of people that have been laid off over the last decade. Ask these people what downsizing feels like.

Your constant concern alone can be a clue to your children that education really is something of importance. You don't have to know theory or philosophy to be a part of your child's education. Keep tabs on their progress. Keep in touch with the teachers to see how things are going. Ask for a copy of the syllabus for the semester. Find out when and what tests are coming up, don't wait for the report card. Many disastrous final grades can be avoided by heading off dangerous trends in the beginning and middle of the semester. You can teach your children many things about being successful at academics without being able to solve a physics problem. Stress to them how important it is that education comes before video games and such. Remind them that there will be no basketball for kids below a certain grade point average. Instill certain habits in them. Remind them that repetition is a key ingredient to any learning process.

Infecting your children with certain values and a hard work ethic can go a long way to becoming an academic powerhouse. What it does is establish a pattern that can be applied to almost any situation regardless of the goal. Think about mathematics for a second. When you are in high school, the purpose of learning trigonometry and calculus is not because when you go to the grocery store you will have to pull out a graphing calculator to determine the cost of the bread. No, the purpose of the mathematical skills is to teach problem solving skills. First, you learn certain laws and formulas. Then different numbers and problems are given to you in many different circumstances. Regardless of how the problems are changed around, if you apply the rules correctly, you should get the correct answer. So what if you do not understand physiology, if you get your children into a firm set of study habits and a strong work ethic, these rules can be applied to any class even if you do not understand the answer to the question. Don't let intimidation and fears ruin your child's future. Just because you are not a law professor at Harvard it does not mean that your child cannot become one.

Verbal encouragement is also a very strong motivator. I did not realize this until I went off to college. When I would come home for the weekend or for semester breaks people were very happy for me and kept me in good spirits. People that I didn't even know very well would come up to me in church and say, "Oh you're the one that is in college, aren't you? Well congratulations, keep up the good work." People were so happy for me, I couldn't believe it. People have said things to me like, "I didn't have the opportunity to go to college, but I am sure glad to see you going. It makes me feel like I'm in college." What this made me realize is that when you are black in this country and you get the opportunity to do something special, you are no longer doing it just for yourself. You are representing so many people that see themselves in you because many of these opportunities are still very new to our race in mass quantities in this country. Verbal encouragement to your children is a very powerful thing. Encourage their success instead of just pointing out when they make mistakes. Let them know that you are supporting them in their dreams.

Become a cheerleader for kids and their education. Don't be intimidated if you weren't a straight 'A' student. Don't feel out of place demanding better even if you weren't able to achieve it. In sports, the cheerleaders are not good at the sports they are cheering for, but that does not stop them though. They are there to motivate the players and encourage them on to victory.

So what you didn't go to college, this should not stop you from wanting that to be a goal for your children. Not many sports players have parents that played professional sports, but that did not stop them. It did not stop these kids from pursuing a goal that is extremely difficult to obtain. Nor did it stop many of these parents from showing up at every game, home or away, to encourage and support their children in what they saw to be a great opportunity for success for their children. I am trying to stress to you that education can be a great opportunity for success for your children, don't hesitate to cheer them on just because you never got to play.

When things would get tough in those first two years of college I wanted to quit but I couldn't. All I could think about was all those people back at home that were pulling for me. I could only remember all of the pats on the back and the encouragement. There was no way that I was going to go back home as a failure. I was not going to reinforce anyone's doubts about us, whether internal or external.

We have to be very careful about what we do around our children and the ideas and the attitudes that we instill in them. How many times have you heard the story told about a young man that grew up watching his father physically abuse his mother only to grow up being abusive to women? The things that we do and the things that we say, whether we are conscious of them or not, can be passed on to our children. How many times have you heard adults in conversations about young children say things like, "He's going to be a pro-ball player." "Look how tall he is." "He's going to have his way with the ladies." If we are honest, we have heard these things said over and over and over in the presence of small children. "Look how pretty she is, she is going to have men wrapped around her finger." We are very quick to tell a young man that he will be a star athlete some day, which is definitely a possibility. We should be just as quick to tell that young man that he could be the person that develops the cure for AIDS. We should tell our daughters that she would look great as a judge and not just encourage her to date and marry a judge.

"Life and Death are in the Power of the Tongue", speak encouraging things to your children. Tell them just how awesome they are. Tell them how brilliant they are. Tell them how smart they are.

Dr. Ben Carson is a very successful neurosurgeon that was born and raised in Detroit, Michigan. His story is absolutely amazing. He was raised by a single mother and they had very little money. He went from being called 'Dumb Carson' and getting the worst grades in the class to being educated at Yale, The University of Michigan, and Johns Hopkins. That is an impressive resume. However, it was not his accomplishments that stood out the most to me when I read his story. What stands out the most to me are the lengths his mother went through to encourage his education.

Dr. Carson's mother was not highly educated. As a matter of fact she could not even read. To encourage her two boys to read she would sit down next to them as they read. She would have a book in her hands turning pages just as if she was reading. She went to great lengths to pretend to be reading just to lead by example to her boys.

Imagine how difficult this really must have been. Just try it one day. Pick up a book that you are not reading and have no intentions on reading. Just browse the words and turn the pages very slowly. I promise you that you will become quickly weary of this task. This woman went to great lengths to encourage the education of her children. Not being able to read is proof that she never mastered academics. This did not stop her from doing what she could to motivate and encourage her children to master academics. Now one of her sons is a famous surgeon.

Parents are responsible for the leadership of their children and we are here to guide them. They look to us for guidance and instruction. The parent is required at times to play many roles in our child's lives. A cheerleader is not the only role that we should play when is comes to our kid's education.

We should also be bodyguards of our child's mind. I think that most of us have heard the stories of children being lead into meetings with strangers over the Internet. Many times, these strangers are sick-minded perverts that molest children. The Internet provides boundless amounts of information that has enhanced all of our lives. At the same time, it can provide boundless amounts of information that we would not like our children to be exposed to. Subjects from racism, to how to construct bombs, can be found on the internet. We must be aware of the good as well as the bad parts of information systems that are available to our children, and at the same time police what they are exposed to.

Your child's future is at stake, and you have to take it seriously. Inspect the web sites that they visit. Keep their computer in a visible place so that you can easily see what is going on in their lives. All too often when these horrific stories hit the news, and the parents are interviewed, they state that they were never aware that their child was involved in such deviant behavior.

You have to control what they see on the television. Many destructive and negative images come across the television screen. These types of images and information far outweigh the types of information that can build a solid foundation for their future. Along with the limitless potential of your child's mind also comes extreme impressionability. Your child's mind is clay to be molded. It can be molded in a good way or it can be molded in a bad way. Who will be the potter of the clay?

My parents have instilled many great things in me. Although neither of my parents have advanced education, there are still many things that they have taught me that have had a great impact on my life even today.

My father never said much when it came to things like school. He taught me the importance of a strong work ethic and doing a good job all of the time.

Most of the things that I have learned from my father I've learned by watching him. Not necessarily things that he discussed directly with me. For example, I have never seen a shut-off notice show up at our house when I was younger. I have never picked up the phone and heard a bill collector on the other line. I have never seen my father intoxicated. I have never seen my father call in and take a day off from work. My father never broke his word to me. Whatever he promised me, he came through with it. I have never seen him put his hands on my mother.

I've found myself falling into the exact mold as my father without him ever verbally telling me to do so. I know that this is because of the environment that he placed around me.

My mother was the one that did all of the talking. My mother would never let me say, "I can't". She would say things like, "Find out how." When I told her that I didn't know how to spell a word, she made me go and get a dictionary to find out how to spell the word. Even today, I laugh at people who tell me that I can't. It is genuinely humorous to me. Because in my mind, I honestly cannot fail. I will be the only hindrance to my success. If I really want it, there is no question that I can have it.

I am thankful for what my parents have instilled in me, and I know for a fact that I have benefited from it. So as parents, please make it a point to encourage and instill greatness in our children. Success is a team sport.

Many people say things like, "I wonder what the future holds?" As a parent you see the future everyday. You walk side by side with the future everyday. You send the future off to school everyday. The children are the future and what you put in them may affect us all. You have the power to change the future so be careful with it, I may have to depend on your child one day.

CHAPTER 16

Now That You Have It, What are You Going to do With It?

"And the valedictorian for the class of 200_ is Mr. /Ms. _____." Everyone is on their feet and applauding. Your family members have tears in their eyes because they are so proud of you. Your big day is finally here. They realize that you may be on a path to change the world. You are a beautiful site to see with your cap and gown on.

After the ceremony is completed you leave with family and friends to eat a nice meal at a great restaurant. This is a very special day in your life. Graduation is an exciting time for everyone involved. On that day you feel like the world is in your palms and your possibilities are limitless.

Now that your future is ahead of you, what will it contain? Do you expect to change the world by going to work for some big company? Do you expect to become wealthy sitting in your cubicle forty hours a week? Do you expect to be respected now by mainstream society? Do you expect to get the best seats and service at restaurants, and for people to stand at attention when you walk into a car dealership? Are you now better than your uneducated brothers and sisters? Are you too good to hang out in your old neighborhood now? What can and can't education do for you?

Education affects many different people in many different ways. Let's talk about money first. Education will definitely afford you a greater salary in many instances when compared to workers that do not have formal education beyond high school. The September 2001 issue of Money magazine states that the average salary for a high school graduate is $26,312 compared to $43,316 for a college graduate. Over the course of a lifetime, this difference can amount to significant sums of money. So now that you are making more money than you've ever made in the past, does this translate into wealth for you? To be honest with you, probably not. The reason is that many of us who obtain education, white or black, follow the road preached to us. GO TO SCHOOL SO THAT YOU CAN GET A GOOD JOB. No one took the time to tell us that almost no one in this country becomes wealthy by working for someone else. Yet we are encouraged to join the ranks of millions of other employees in this country and beg someone else to put us on their payroll. Getting on someone's payroll gives you a salary, it does not make you wealthy. This salary is usually just enough to supply us with things. It does not give us financial security.

We prepare our resumes and put on our best dark suits, hoping to find the approval of the person interviewing us. We rehearse and practice our answers to possible interview questions over and over. At this point many of us have no clue that this scenario is very unlikely to fulfill the financial goals that we would like to achieve for ourselves and our families. All we know is that now we can afford a more expensive car and nicer clothes. So we jump on the never ending treadmill of more expensive things and credit card debt that we can never seem to pay off. Big ticket items are mere symbols of wealth only, they do not represent true wealth. As the years go by, we have accumulated more stuff but no true wealth. We fool ourselves into believing that when our salary increases, then we will save more money. What really happens is that as our salary increases the price tag of the things we purchase also increases, but we never actually get ahead financially.

It is not the formal education that leads to wealth. There are thousands of people in this country that have multiple college degrees but could not survive for a month if they lost their jobs. Just having a college education alone will not bring you wealth. On the other hand it is not a lack of formal university education that leads to poverty. Bill Gates dropped out of college and concentrated on his dream and now he is one of the richest men in the world. A large contributor to wealth is what you choose to do with what you earn and what you learn. Wealthy people don't work for the company. Wealthy people own the company.

So don't just settle for a good job and make another person rich, make yourself rich. This allows you to empower others. Someone very close to me went to college and obtained a degree in computer science. They make a good salary for a four-year degree by working for a local company. Bill Gates didn't finish college and owns one of the most powerful computer companies in the world. He recently gave millions of dollars to the United Negro College Fund. Are you starting to get my point? Because of ownership, he is in the position to empower others.

Most of the wealthy people in America work for themselves or have ownership of what they produce. They don't get up every morning to punch someone else's clock. Their time and talents go into planting seeds for their own future harvest. The person that is incorporated with his own business has financial advantages that the common worker will never enjoy while being an employee. If you are blessed to know someone personally that is wealthy, I am willing to bet you that they don't work for someone else. "But the idea of owning a business is scary." No, being 60 years old at the time Enron collapsed is scary. Being forced to live on social security is scary.

It is time to wake up and see what is happening around us. Very large corporations are downsizing everyday. When this happens, hundreds of people lose their jobs and they lose what they thought was job security. As long as you work for someone else, you have no job security, no matter what they tell you and no matter what they pay you. When their need for you is over, you are thrown to the side like yesterday's newspaper. When they release you, they don't care if your children's college education is paid for or whether or not you have funded your retirement. They don't care if your mortgage is paid off, nor do they care how many car payments you have remaining.

What I want you to understand the most is that your education, whether formal or not, won't protect you from downsizing. So don't think that because you went to some big-time university that you are secure and protected because it is just not true. The days of 'go to school and get a good job' are over, and anyone believing it is making a big mistake. If you are not willing to break away from this old way of thinking, then you run the risk of financial hardship.

How many times have you gone to fast food restaurants and grocery stores and have seen people old enough to be your grandparents working there? If you start to pay attention to it the next time you are out what you will find will be quite shocking to you. You will start to see that it is actually very common to see people that should be retired working at these or similar places. Do you think that these people enjoy their occupations? Fifty years ago, do you think that this is how these people envisioned themselves living out the final years of their lives? No, of course not. These people are working these jobs because they have no choice. Financially they are in bad shape. Many of them, after retiring, or after the death of a spouse, realized that social security is not enough to live on, and they must go back to work. Work for themselves this time? No. They go back and again work for someone else. The same situation that brought them no financial success in the first place.

Trust me, when you get old, the last thing you want to be doing is bagging groceries next to some teenager. You must take your future into your own hands and not depend on the government or some company to do it for you. "Can I get fries with that please?" In the year 2001, Chrysler made the announcement that 27,000 workers were going to be laid off. This number included blue and white-collar workers. These workers had no reason to feel that their future was in question. They were employed by one of the largest corporations in the world. A corporation that had some of the hottest products in their industry at the time of the announcement. In a segment of time when SUV'S were one of the most popular automobiles around, they could barely keep up with demand. Their Jeep Grand Cherokee was selling like hot cakes. This is my point exactly. That even working for a large powerful company with wide selling products does not provide you with financial security. These people never saw it coming and were left out in the cold. This did not just affect the worker on the line with the high school diploma. This layoff spread up into the offices where the blue suit and ties were. Even their fancy college degrees didn't protect them from being released.

What is even more disturbing about this large release of people is when we really analyze how far it may have actually reached. Imagine if each of these 27,000 people represented a head of a family. As a hypothetical situation, say that each family had 2-3 people in it. With this scenario potentially over 50,000 lives could have been affected by this layoff. We must start to take our financial future into our own hands. There is no such thing as a safe and secure job.

Headline, DETROIT NEWS 8/17/01-- "FORD AXES 5000 JOBS." Are you starting to see a pattern here? Or are you going to wait until it is you? Are you going to wait until you get handed the pink slip before you realize that this is real? There is a constant drive to keep profits up and at the same time cut costs. What are some of the costs incurred when running a company? To be quite honest, you are a cost to your company, if you chose to work for one. Your salary and the health insurance that you have costs the company money.

One way to cut costs is to cut people or cut jobs. Do you think that when a company cuts the number of jobs that they also lower the amount of work that is required to be done? Of course not. In many instances, the same amount of production is required by contributions from less people. For the sake of profits, many people's lives are turned upside down by layoffs and firings. The pressure to keep profits up are to make the investors on Wall Street happy.

I do not know what it is like to be the CEO of a fortune 500 company and be pressed with having to make such a decision. However, I do know what it is like to be on the other end of this type of decision. I know what it is like to work for a company and have the false belief of security, only to meet a rude awakening one day. I know what it is like to believe that you have a job as long as you want one, and one day have the manager tell you the opposite. The same guy you worked overtime and weekends for when he asked you to will be the same guy telling you how sorry he is when he has to let you go.

It would be very interesting to speak to the people that have the final say in such decisions. I'm pretty sure that there is much contemplating and many board meetings before such a decision is rendered. But I would really like to know deep down in their hearts if they really care about Jerome.

You know Jerome. He works on the line. He has worked for the company for over ten years or so. He never made it to college. His uncle got him this job. He has never missed a day and he doesn't cause any trouble. He just does his job. When the axe swings, being a loyal employee and a hard worker is not enough to save him. Showing up on time and staying late when asked does not save Jerome either. I want you to learn something from Jerome. I want you to know that you could be the absolute best worker around and still get released when you work for someone else. As long as you leave your future in someone else's hands, this is the risk that you run. The people that let Jerome go can easily make salaries in the six-figure range. They pay more in taxes than Jerome makes in a year.

What about Mike? Ask Mike how he feels. Mike graduated from the University of Michigan. This is one of the higher-ranking schools in the country. They have a top-ten business school. He has his diplomas and awards hanging up in his office. He wears a nice suit and shirt to work everyday. He just bought a nice house in the suburbs. However, none of his possessions and things stops the swing of the axe from hitting him either. He finds himself in a similar situation as Jerome.

Having these credentials, Mike thought that he was protected from such things. On the outside, it would appear that one man is better off than the other. The reality is this, when we relinquish control of our financial future into the hands of someone else, regardless of our educational level, we face the risk of dire consequences.

To become a surgeon in America requires eight years of education after high school and then an additional five to ten years of residency/fellowship specialty training. This at times can amount to about fifteen years of work after high school. This takes us well into our thirties before we even get started. Traditionally, doctors in America have been some of the highest-paid professionals. Many doctors in the past retired very comfortably. With the many changes in the healthcare system in America regarding third parties and reimbursement issues, this is no longer the case for all physicians. Today's doctors are not promised financial security nor are they guaranteed job security. So if a job that is one of the most respected, and one of the most difficult to obtain promises you nothing, then no one is safe and secure. I am just trying to stress to you that going to school and getting a good job does not work anymore, for anyone. No matter how smart you are.

There is a very small segment of the population that becomes wealthy while still working for someone else. Unfortunately, very few of us will fit into this small demographic. Mostly these are CEO's (chief executive officer) of large companies, athletes, and entertainers. CEO's of companies do not always become wealthy because of a large salary that they are paid. They also become wealthy because they are given a percentage of ownership in the company through stock options. These hundreds or thousands of shares of stock multiplied times the price per share, $1 up to hundreds of dollars per share, equals millions of dollars some times. The incentive for these CEO's is to guide the company down a profitable path which will in turn drive up the value of the stock which ultimately makes more money for everyone involved. The key to this relationship is ownership. The CEO's, through the stock options, have partial ownership of the company. Almost no one obtains wealth without ownership.

Athletes and entertainers on the other hand actually are paid very large salaries at times and this allows them to achieve wealth while being an employee. This very small segment of the population obtains wealth without ownership. They are the exception and not the rule. God has blessed very few of us with these abilities, so the rest of us have to choose a different route. As I am writing this book, the highest contract to date is a quarter of a billion dollar baseball contract. So unless you can be like Mike, Jordan or Jackson, you need to go to school and you need more education.

As I previously stated, we fall into the role that has been ingrained into our psyche, GO TO SCHOOL SO THAT YOU CAN GET A GOOD JOB. The majority of millionaires in this country are entrepreneurs, owners of their own businesses. They understand that you will not become wealthy punching someone else's clock. Think about it for a minute, the role that we play. We go to work week after week after week. We give the company all of our efforts and talents and time. We spend our entire working career contributing to someone else's wealth. Some of you work for companies that make profits in the millions, yet they pay you thousands. Our children scramble to get loans for education while the owners of these companies pay their children's tuition up front. We save up all year for a couple of weeks vacation. While our hard hours worked makes profits for the company that sends the owner and his family to spend summers in the South of France. How about you become an owner and make millions and pay out thousands. That sounds like a much better situation to me.

I just have a hard time looking at another man from across the table and allowing him to tell me what I am worth. But that is what we do. Here we are, created by God, with tremendous talents and abilities now enhanced even further with some polish (education), and we let someone with no more power and no more ability determine our future and tell us what we are worth. No one will ever value you like you value yourself. No one will ever adequately compensate you for what you are really worth. They pat us on the heads like children and verbally tell us how much we mean to the company, but this verbal adoration is never manifested in our bank account. When you look in the mirror you should see priceless. Stop letting people put a price tag on you.

I am not saying that you should never work for anyone else at any point in your life. That is not what I am saying. I believe what you should do is obtain as much knowledge and information about an area that interests you first. I recommend that you do go and work for someone or some company in that particular field. This should not be a permanent situation. You should gain as much experience and as many contacts as you can from this experience. After you have made the proper relationships and have gathered adequate knowledge, you should be ready to go off to take your future into your own hands and no longer be at the mercy of someone else.

This is the road that will take you to wealth. Incorporating their energy and their talents into producing for their own family is what the wealthy people of America do. Wealthy people do not spend 100% of their energy contributing to someone else's future. If just having a job is your goal, then the majority of graduates will be happy after obtaining their education. The sad thing is that many of these graduates will get a very rude awakening when the company that valued them so much moves jobs out of the country and starts to downsize and their position is eliminated.

I am presenting this information to you just so that you can make informed decisions. You need to know what the reality is. You need to decide what the best situation is for you.

There are other freedoms, besides finances, that are

available to the person who works for themselves. Being your own boss makes it easier for you to maintain your integrity. Many unfair business practices and unethical business decisions are made everyday in the name of making higher profits. I have a hard time believing that every person behind every one of these shady decisions are inherently evil people. I believe that they are good people that have just made bad decisions. Pressure from higher ranking officials in the company causes people to do things that they would not ordinarily do. The hopes of advancing their careers and wanting to be looked at as a 'team player' causes people to do things that they would not ordinarily do. The pressure to live a certain lifestyle and the need for more money causes people to do things that they would not ordinarily do. Pressure can lead people to compromise their integrity.

What you must understand is that at the end of the day you will have to live with every choice that you've made. When it is all over, you are the one ultimately responsible for every action that you take. You are the one that will be held accountable for what you do, not your boss. Why not be your own boss?

What kind of problems can education cause for you? Sometimes it can cause social problems. Unfortunately some of our brothers and sisters start to change when they are no longer working in the mailroom. They start to think that they are better than everyone else and don't have to say "Good morning" anymore. This is a very unfortunate circumstance that tends to divide us at times. Are you going to allow your success to separate you from your people? Or are you going to be an example that shows our confused youth that we can all succeed?

As the gap in America widens between the rich and the poor, this is even more apparent in the black community. With the changes in this country over the last forty to fifty years, there has been a small segment of black America that has catapulted from middle class to the higher society. This at times has caused resentment from both groups towards each other. The successful individuals at times can say things like, "I did it, why can't you make it." The individuals that have been left behind at times can say things like, "He/She thinks that they are better than everybody else." Sometimes it is so obvious that you can palpate the tension when the two groups are in the same area like a cafeteria or some other mutual location.

This is definitely something that needs to be overcome. Division among us will certainly not lead to success as a whole. Maybe sometimes some among us have to be big enough to take the first step to make the situation work. Instead of letting the tension build up, be the first person to say "Good morning". Regardless if the other person sees you everyday without saying anything. If we never make ourselves available, how can we be a help to anyone?

Now that you have it, what are you going to do with it? Are you going to turn your nose up at those that have not achieved what you have? Or are you going to be willing to take the knowledge that you have and share that knowledge with others so that maybe they can achieve what you have? Come on be honest with me, now that you have it, what are you really going to do with it? Are you going to hide out there in that nice home, and drive back and forth in your BMW, and never try to make a difference in anyone's life except your own? *To Whom Much is Given, Much is Required.*

CHAPTER 17

Now That You Have It, What Are You Going To Do With It? Part II

In the previous chapter we touched on a few scenarios concerning what you could do with the education that you receive. I wanted to stress to you that whatever you do in the way of education, please maximize it to your benefit, and the benefit of your family. If you use all of your productive years making someone else rich, you will be very disappointed when it is time for you to retire.

Use your skills and knowledge to build a legacy for your family. Spend your productive years sowing into your own wealth. Ensure that your children will not have to take out business loans when it is their turn to embark on this journey of success. Ensure that their college education will be paid for so that they don't start off their adult lives behind a mountain of debt like I had to start out after college.

With more education and with more success comes more money. Now that you have the money, what do you do with it? It is not enough to just make money. When you don't have any money, it may seem that this alone would be adequate, just to have more money. What becomes very apparent after you start to make more money is that you don't seem to accumulate more money, you just buy more expensive things with the money that you have. We buy more expensive automobiles, we eat at better restaurants, and we wear more expensive clothes when we start to make more money.

You can make all the money that your heart desires, but if you don't use is wisely, you can still die broke. We have all heard countless stories of athletes and entertainers that have made millions of dollars, but at the end they were completely broke. How can you make so much money and have absolutely nothing to show for it? Once again we go back to the theme of the whole book, education. We must become more educated in the realm of business and finance to be a complete success. This is where some of these athletes and entertainers have failed themselves. They had no problem making the money, but as we hear time and time again, many of them obviously have had a problem keeping the money. You must be educated in order to make it in today's world. There is no substitute and there is no way around it. Yes, you can make the money, but can you hold on to the money?

Over the next few chapters we will briefly touch on the subject of money. It is by no way all inclusive. As a matter of fact it is quite basic. I just want to introduce you to some very important concepts that were taught to me and have blessed me. Do not substitute these next few chapters for your financial education. This is by no way all of what you need to know. This is just a very basic introduction to wet your appetite.

You need to subscribe to a magazine with money or invest-ing and finance as the subject. This will constantly keep you focused on the proper handling and management of your money. You need to go and get a financial planner. You need someone to sit down with you, one on one, and listen to your long term goals so they can help you formulate a plan for yourself. We go to the doc-tor for medical advice. Some of us go to lawyers for legal advice. Your finances are very important and you need to talk to a profes-sional regarding financial advice.

As important as money is to our lives and our lifestyles it seems strange to me how few of us get professional advice regard-ing money. When you add the fact of how few of us are wealthy it is really puzzling to me how few of us seek advice about money. One of my greatest assets is that I am humble enough to admit that I don't know everything that I need to know. I learned a long time ago that the most successful people surround themselves with peo-ple that are smarter and more talented than there are. If you are going to accumulate wealth then you are going to have to start to get advice from someone that knows more about it than you do.

Do not let this be all though. This is your money. Don't just get a financial planner and completely turn your financial future over to them. You need to be educated also. Start at the book store and pick up some books to help you get started. As a physician I try to get people to take control of their own health and to have a better understanding of it. If they have a better understanding of it, they can contribute to their own well being. I can do nothing for a patient that is not willing to take an active role in their health. A financial planner can do nothing for you, if you do not take responsibility for your own wealth. You may even have to hire and fire a few of them until you get one that is meeting your specific needs and that is o.k.

There are some things in life that are constants, where cer-tain conditions are met regardless of the season and regardless of the situation. As I told you before we should concentrate on pat-terns of success and not patterns of failure. If we are going to han-dle our money properly, we should pattern ourselves after people that have a lot of it, rich people, and not after broke people. There are a few concepts across the board that many rich people subscribe to. These are constants in the circles of the rich.

There are a few questions that we should answer considering these constants. 1) What is wealth and are you wealthy? 2) Why do rich people invest? 3) When do rich people invest? 4) Where do rich people invest?

Once again these next few chapters are only very brief introductions to your financial education. You cannot stop here if you plan to make smart decisions when it comes to your money.

CHAPTER 18

What is Wealth and Are You Wealthy?

What is wealth? Webster's dictionary says: 1) valuable and large material possessions; riches 2) profusion; abundance 3) all property.

Many of us walk around with the wrong idea of what wealth is. I do not know where these false ideas came from, but wherever it started, it has poisoned many of our minds with the wrong information. Some of us think that if a person makes a large salary then that automatically means that that person is wealthy. There are countless upon countless numbers of people that have made lots of money in their lifetime that still are not wealthy.

A large salary does not always equate with wealth. Although it does give you more leverage in an attempt to accumulate wealth, it does not in and of itself make you wealthy. There are some people that assume that if a person is making over $100,000 per year then they will eventually become rich. I know people that make over $200,000 per year and are not rich. How can this be? How can you make so much money and not become wealthy? Pay attention. Do you know what many people that make $200,000 per year typically do with the money that they make? Many times they have over $200,000 worth of bills. Many of them live in $300,000 or $400,000 homes. Some of them are driving eighty thousand dollar cars. Their kids go to the most expensive schools and they take elaborate vacations. As you can see, $200,000 is eaten up pretty quickly when we spend it like this. There is absolutely nothing wrong with this. It just happens to be the opposite of how you should handle your money when you are trying to make it grow for you. Remember, the goal is not to work your entire life just to make money and buy things. The goal is to eventually get to a point where your money is making money for you. When your money is making money for you, it allows you to become involved in other things besides just making money. It gives you freedom, and there is nothing like freedom.

So a large salary does not necessarily make you a wealthy person. As you can see, it is possible to make a nice salary and still not accumulate wealth. There are obviously other components that must be involved besides making a lot of money. It is not always what or how much you make, but what you do with what you make. I have found myself in interesting situations at times while in various stores. I pay for something and the cashier forgets to give me my five cents back. When I politely remind the clerk about my change I have been asked, "You really want your five cents?" "Yes," I reply. "Rich people didn't get rich by throwing all of their money away, they get rich by accumulating money." The response is usually a puzzled look on the person's face. Many of them don't understand it because most of us don't understand money. We understand how to spend it, but we don't really understand how wealth and money really works.

We need to look at wealth the way that rich people look at wealth. You would be surprised to know that many millionaires have a small salary. Most of the millionaires in this country are entrepreneurs, owners of their own small business. The definition of a small business is one that has less than four-hundred employees. These people hold their wealth inside of the companies that they own or other assets that they own. Because they own the company, they own the wealth of the company. They pay themselves a small salary and many other things that they need are bought through the company. This is an example of how knowledge puts you on another level of society.

The laptop computer that I am writing this book on was purchased through one of the companies that I own, as a legitimate business expense. While many of you pay full price for things like laptop computers, for me it is a legitimate business expense, and I pay a fraction of what you pay. This allows me to accumulate wealth over the course of my life because it decreases my taxable income and frees up my dollars for other things.

Taxes are one of our greatest expenses. For every dollar that we make, the government takes 30 to 40 cents of it in income taxes. Off of the top, before you even feed your own children, the government is in your pocket. Thirty to forty percent is bad enough if this was all, but it isn't. Then we are charged sales tax when we purchase things. We are charged property taxes on our homes, city and county where I live. Did you make a profit on your stocks last year? Good, because now you are going to pay capital gains taxes. Even when we die our estate is taxed, if it is not properly protected. You would think that after paying taxes all of our lives that we would be rewarded for being caring enough and smart enough to leave things for our children, but the truth is that we are taxed again. We are taxed again on money that we were already taxed on as an income tax. Estate taxes can be as high as fifty percent at times. When you die, one-half of your estate can and will be taken from your children if you are not properly protected.

One way to increase profits is to decrease expenses. To increase your profits you need to decrease one of your greatest expenses, taxes. This is one of the greatest reasons to put your talents to work to make yourself wealthy and not someone else, because it allows you to decrease your tax burden the greatest and it is not only allowed but encouraged by your own government. Currently, President Bush is attempting to increase the business deduction to seventy-five thousand dollars. This seventy-five thousand dollar deduction will not be available to the employee, it will only be available to corporations. By incorporating, many things that you purchase can be purchased as a business expense and deducted on your taxes. The key to this whole idea is that these items are purchased with pre-tax dollars, and not after tax dollars, which is typical for most Americans. Employees work, the government takes, and they can only spend what is left over. Corporations make money, spend money, and then are taxed only on what is left over. See the following example.

Employee
1) Income = $100,000
2) 30-40% tax on $100,000
3) $60,000 left over to spend

Corporations
1)	Income = $100,000
2)	Spend $80,000
3)	Taxed on only $20,000

In the above example you can see that there is a significant difference in spending power and how much of your money is taxed when you use your talents to work for you through corporations. This is how the rich operate. This is not how the poor operate. The rich protect themselves through corporations and increase their wealth by decreasing their taxes. The poor work harder and harder and are taxed more and more.

This is not rocket science. This is where our school system and our parents and our grandparents have failed us. No one has taken the time to teach us about wealth and finance. The only thing that people ever teach you is how to make money. No one tells us how to keep the money. Anyone can make money. I have been making money since the sixth grade when I had a paper route. It is really no big deal. The winners are those that are able to keep their money.

What are some other misconceptions about money? We also tend to think that when we see people in fancy cars or wearing fancy clothes that they are wealthy. This is not necessarily the case. We must change this perception about wealth. Having expensive things does not equate with wealth. We really seem to have this problem very bad in the black community.

How many times in the black community do we see a Cadillac parked in the driveway of a rundown home? You know, and I know, that we see it all of the time. It makes absolutely no sense at all, but we continue to perpetuate this foolishness generation after generation. As blacks, some of us are more content with just having the symbols of wealth rather than true wealth itself. Some of us are more content with the expensive clothes and cars, than having our accounts bursting at the seams. It is because we do not have a true understanding of what wealth really is. We spend our whole life chasing after things and when we die, the next generation is no better off than we were because we have left them nothing to build upon.

Black people, we must wake up and discontinue this cycle of poverty and ignorance in our community. How many times have you seen this scenario played out? A black person dies and the family comes around asking for donations because there is not enough money to bury the person. You mean to tell me that a person can live fifty or sixty years on this planet and not even accumulate enough money for their body to be properly buried?

Let's assume that they had a super-duper funeral that cost $10,000. Let's assume that the deceased worked from age 20 to age 60. If this person would have just accumulated the average of $1.50/day, it would have been enough to pay for the funeral. The cycle repeats over and over and we leave nothing behind for our families but debt. We can never expect to progress as a people if we start from the same place as previous generations. This is not progress. I don't know a single black person that has inherited anything of substantial financial significance. Not one. This must change.

How do rich people look at wealth? Many wealthy people do not look at how expensive their watch is or their clothes to determine if they are well off. Many wealthy people use a term called Net Worth. It is a financial snap shot that gives you a true picture of where you are in terms of your over all financial health. This is how some rich people determine if they are at the level that they want to be. They do not determine their financial success by how expensive their car is. How do you determine your net worth?

To simplify things, your net worth is your assets minus your liabilities. Webster defines assets as anything advantageous. In financial terms, these are things of value. Liabilities are things that you owe or need to pay back. Let's take a look at the following example over on the next page.

Here is a simplified version, your financial planner will take you into much more detail.

ASSETS

Bank Accounts (checking, savings, money markets)

$_____

Stocks, Bonds, Mutual funds, other investments
i.e.   Real estate

$_____

Current Appraised value of home

$_____

Value of Auto

$_____

401k or other investment vehicles

$_____
$_____ = Total assets

LIABILITIES

All of your current bills, including credit cards

$_____

Mortgage owed

$_____

Automobile loans

$_____

Student loans (ouch)

$_____

Any other outstanding loans

$_____
$_____= Total liabilities

Now take the total assets and subtract total liabilities and this will tell you your net worth. This is how you will really know how you are doing. This is a lot more information than a salary, or how much you can afford to pay for a pair of shoes will ever give you. This is a true picture of your financial health, and it will really wake you up when it comes to your finances. It was a real eye opener the first time I did mine years ago. It showed me that I was in much worse financial shape than I realized. At times, things can be much worse than they seem, and we need to know where we are starting from if we are to make a successful journey.

The first time I calculated my net worth it was a negative value. I cannot tell you how shocked I was. It hurt my feelings a little bit. I knew that I wasn't rich, but I had no idea how bad off I really was. But if I had never done it, I would have continued to walk around with a false sense of security. After I learned what my net worth was, it showed me that I had a long way to go to get to financial security.

Many of us are walking around with a false sense of security. We think that because we can drive a nice car and live in a nice house that we are doing well. We think that because we can afford to eat out, and we take vacations every year that we have it going on. This is not necessarily the case. We need to do an in-depth analysis of our finances. If we do not know where we are now, then how are we going to get to where we want to be? Because I could afford the things that I enjoyed, I thought that I was doing o.k. and I was wrong. Once again let's look at the example on the next page.

Let's go through an example of calculating net worth.

ASSETS

$500 = Bank Accounts (checking, savings, money markets)

$0 = Stocks, Bonds, Mutual funds, other investments i.e. Real estate

$150,000 = Current Appraised value of home (primary residence)

$20,000 = Value of Auto

$0 = 401k or other investment vehicles

$170,500 = Total Assets

LIABILITIES

$10,000 =All of your current bills, including credit cards

$140,000 = Mortgage owed

$27,000 = Automobile loans

$20,000 = Student loans (ouch)

$10,000 = Any other outstanding loans i.e. home equity loans

$207,000 = Total liabilities

ASSETS MINUS LIABILITIES = NET WORTH = (-$36,500)

Many people in America are living with numbers similar to

these and their homes are going without lack. Because we are able to afford the things that we like, we don't see the need for concern. Many of us don't recognize the problem until it is too late.

This goes back to our lack of financial education. Many of us still feel this way. We think that if we can afford the things that we like, then we are financially stable. Why do you think that when you go to the store they have posted in bold print, "ONLY $19/MONTH", for something that costs $400? They are playing on your ignorance. They know that in your mind you're going to say, "Only $19, that's nothing, I can easily afford that payment." In the end you pay three times what it cost you with interest added.

Going back to the above equation will show you how to fix the situation. To increase your net worth you need to increase the numbers in the asset column and decrease the numbers in the liability column. That is the key to wealth in a nut shell. Rich people have more assets than liabilities. Poor people have more liabilities than assets. Spend more of your time building assets.

If you want to be financially secure, then you need to see things the way financially secure people see things. They determine their position by their net worth, not by whether or not they can make the payment each month. Not by how much their home costs or by how much their car costs. Wake up and try it. Calculate your net worth and find out if you are where you need to be. Stop equating wealth with how much stuff you have, that is how broke people think. Broke people focus on their things. Rich people focus on net worth. If you focus your energy on getting the wealth first, you can buy as much stuff as you want. The problem is that many of us buy the stuff first, and we never accumulate wealth because we spend our entire lives paying for the stuff.

CHAPTER 19

WHY DO RICH PEOPLE INVEST?

Let's stick to the theme. If you want something then I believe that you would be quite safe trying to pattern yourself after someone that has already done what you are trying to do. We know that working and making money is not enough, and we know that we must have our money work for us. There has to be something about this investing thing. Why is investing such a constant activity when it comes to the rich? They all invest in something, but why do they do it?

The reason that they do it is quite simple. It is so simple, but many of us fail to recognize it. In fact many of us can work our entire life time and never know it until someone explains it to us and opens our eyes. This is once again why it is so important to be careful of who we surround ourselves with because we need to be with people that are going somewhere. These are the people that can teach us things that may change our lives.

What have the rich learned that many of us will never figure out? They have learned that getting paid only for the hours worked will never amount to significant sums of money. If the only money that you ever receive comes in proportion to the hours that you have worked the previous week, then I doubt that you will ever become wealthy. When you start to associate with people that have more than you, and know more than you, it will open your mind up to an entirely different set of possibilities.

Most of us are still chained to our jobs. I say chained because we cannot leave when we want to. Something that is chained does not have freedom of movement. The minute we stop working is the very minute we stop getting paid, and because of this we cannot afford to stop working. This is not how the rich make their money. The rich make money when they are working and when they are not working. That is one of the reasons that they invest. Investing brings money in while you are sleeping and playing. Investing brings money in while you are on vacation. Why do you think rich people are always smiling and everyday-workers are always complaining? Rich people are smiling because having money is fun. Spending money is fun. Everyday workers complain all of the time but they rarely leave. If they hate it so much then why do they stay? Because they know that the minute that they leave will be the very minute that they stop getting paid.

Let's take a moment and look at compound interest. Compound interest is so amazing that some people have called it the 'eighth wonder of the world'. With compound interest, not only is the initial amount of your investment put away for you, but a percentage of the total investment is added to your initial investment depending on the rate of return that you receive. This is repeated on a regular basis again and again and again. So if you make a

$10,000 investment and you make a 10% profit on it, then your new total is $11,000. You may say that $1000 isn't much, but remember what you did to get it. It wasn't based on getting up and going to work. You didn't make the $1000 after having to hear your boss scream and complain all week. You didn't have to work overtime and double shifts to make this extra $1000. It is not about just working harder but also about working smarter and having your money work for you. You made that $1000 while you were sitting on the couch eating ice cream or watching television.

Remember that this can get repeated over and over again. The next time you make a 10% profit it is based on an investment of $11,000 instead of only $10,000. With the new 10% profit, your new total is now $12,100. This occurs whether you show up to work or not. This is not predicated on how many hours you worked last week. This is a nice deal don't you think. With compound interest, you get back more than you put in. With hourly wages, you get back only what you put in. To be honest with you, I feel that you get back less than what you put in because no one is ever going to pay you what you are really worth. You are priceless, don't ever forget that. I believe that I am worth much much more than $30,000 or $40,000 dollars per year, what about you?

Now do you see why investing is a universal activity among the rich? Many of them do it because it allows your finances to be multiplied many times over. Even while you are playing this occurs.

I will not dive deeply into the many possible investment vehicles from stocks, bonds, and mutual funds, futures, real estate, CD's, money markets, and precious metals. This is where you step in and start to learn what is right for you, in addition to talking to a financial planner. You cannot just let your funds sit in a savings or checking account. If you ever expect to accumulate any significant amount of money, you must go out and plant your seeds in fertile ground and watch them grow. Checking and savings accounts are not going to produce a very large harvest for you.

Look at your monthly checking or savings statement the next time that it comes. For one, they are paying you a very minimal rate of interest, especially in today's economy. You are probably getting

2-3% interest. This won't keep up with inflation, even if you actually received it. You never end up seeing this money by the time the bank charges you all of the fees that they require to hold your money. Money of yours that they use to make money for themselves by lending it out. They hold your money for you and pay you 2-3% interest. They turn around and loan your money to someone else at a rate of up to 15% at times.

Let me get this straight. I'm going to let you hold my money for me. While you are holding my money for me, you lend it out and use it to make money for yourself and then you charge me fees to hold my money. The bank manager says, "You are absolutely correct." And we give him our money anyway. They lull us into this by disguising it with the interest that they are supposed to pay us. What happens is that you never see this money because of all of the fees that they charge you. By the time they charge you ATM fees, minimum balance fees, check writing fees and so on and so on, you actually end up paying them. Wake up people. Wealthy people do not have the majority of their funds lying around in a checking or savings account. They already realize that this is not a profit making venture.

Wealthy people look for continuous streams of income. You won't become wealthy if you are only paid for the hours that you have put in. There are only twenty-four of them in a day and working more than eight in a day gets old very quickly. Your favorite recording artist gets a percentage of every CD sold. This percentage is called royalties. It doesn't matter if they are performing tonight or not, they get paid. No matter if they record another album, as long as the records already produced sells, they get paid. They get paid when they are sleeping and they get paid when they are awake. This is the kind of income that you want. You don't want to only rely on getting paid for the hours that you work.

A man that owns an apartment building gets rent checks coming to him at the beginning of every month, like clock work. It doesn't matter what else he chooses to do, he has income coming in that has no reflection on his hours worked. Get your mind away from the hourly wage mentality. This is not the mentality of the rich.

I found out a long time ago that if something is being given away very easily then it must not be worth very much. Hourly wage jobs are not hard to come by. This should tell you something about its true value.

CHAPTER 20

WHEN DO RICH PEOPLE INVEST?

Timing, timing, timing. There is timing to everything. There is also timing to investing. This is not just a random thing that you should do. It is not timed with the seasons, or based on the position of the sun and the solar system, but it is very precise and calculated. Before you get discouraged by this just hold on and be patient. I am not about to tell you that you have to be some professional stock analyst or market guru in order to get rich. This is not what I mean when I talk about the timing of investments.

So what is the timing of the rich, and when do rich people

invest? It is once again a simple concept. It is not some compli-cated mathematical formula that comes up with a date on a calen-dar. Quite simply, the rich invest first. First you say? When is first? Do you mean the first of the month, or maybe the first of the year? Not necessarily so. Just plain first. Rich people invest first before they do anything else. They take it off the top. Wealthy people have taken their time and their talents and deposited them into assets for themselves. First, not last. The wealthy deposit into their own futures first before anyone else's.

On your quest to accumulate wealth, it may help you to adopt a concept called 'PAY YOURSELF FIRST'. You must take your future into your own hands. Your hands and not someone else's hands. Your grandparents had social security from the government waiting for them when they retired. You and I do not have that lux-ury. For one, the amount of money received from social security is not enough to live a comfortable life. Why do you think that you see people retire and then go right back to work? They do it because social security is not enough to make it. The second problem is that there is no guarantee that social security will even be available when you and I become old enough to receive it.

With that dim picture, you would be a fool to believe that social security is all that you are going to need to support you and your family when you become elderly. Take your future into your own hands. Pay yourself first and guarantee that there will be finances waiting for you when you retire. Insure yourself a pleasant retirement. Not one filled with eating TV dinners and working part-time at the mall to make ends meet.

Some of you may say, "Well, the company that I work for has an excellent retirement plan." When Enron collapsed, many people lost their retirement plans. One of the largest companies in America folded and the people working there lost it all. Why? Because their future was in the hands of the CEO and the board of directors. This is a possible outcome when your future is entrusted with someone else. No one cares about your family as much as you do. Don't expect someone else to have their best interests in mind.

Paying yourself first is simply taking a percentage of all of your earnings and investing them first. Off of the top. Not after you pay your bills. Not after you do all of the other things that you consider important. You should value yourself too much to pay everybody else first.

You should hold yourself and your children in much higher regard than you hold the gas company or the light company. But we will break our necks to pay our cellular phone bill and worry less about paying ourselves first. I promise you these things are very important. You must pay your gas bill and your light bill, I understand this. I am not telling you to neglect your responsibilities. A cell phone in the past was a luxury. I have become so busy that for me it has become a necessity. I cannot stop at a payphone every time someone needs to speak to me. I am not telling you to stop paying this bill. What I am telling you is that if you pay yourself first, you will find a way to pay those other bills.

You will find a way to pay those other bills even if it means that you have to cut back in a few areas. What we tend to do is pay all of our bills first, and if there is anything left over then we may put some money away for our future. Well, in reality what usually happens? What happens is that at the end of the month there is nothing left over to pay ourselves with, or invest. So we put it off until the next month and then the next month and so on. Before we know it, years have gone by and we have accumulated nothing. All of our bills are paid, but we have accumulated nothing.

When you die, who do you expect to be at your funeral? Do you expect the phone company to send a card to your family saying how sorry they are in their time of grief? Do you think the gas or electric company will be sitting in the audience at the funeral? They should be. Right? For your whole life you were such a good customer. You paid all of your bills on time and they made tons of money off of you. They will be at your funeral to say goodbye. Right? Wrong. When you die, these companies that you were so loyal to won't be there to pay their respects.

Your family will be there. Your children will be there. The ones that you have the greatest obligation to will be there. In our lifetime we will have paid hundreds of thousands into the pockets of these companies and many of us will leave absolutely nothing to our children. How backwards is this? The ones that we love the most get the absolute least from all our efforts.

You must pay yourself first if you have any hopes of accumulating wealth. A portion of everything that you receive must be put away for your future and your children's future. Remember the unsuccessful farmer? The unsuccessful farmer ate all of his seeds. What kind of harvest do you think that he will have? Do not put these companies before yourself and your children.

Once again, I am not telling you to shun your obligation to pay your bills. What I am saying is change your priority of who gets paid and when. I personally even take it a step further and give on a regular basis to my local church organization. I consider this an investment in and of itself. So even before I pay into my personal investment fund, I pay into the church. We must take care of the most important groups in our life first. When it comes to yourself, you have to become selfish in some regards. I know your parents told you to always be considerate. In most aspects I agree. But when it comes to investing and saving for your future, you must pay yourself first.

Can I be honest with you? I don't really trust you to pay yourself first. I just don't believe that you have the discipline to do this. Can I tell you something else? I don't trust myself either. When I was working for a large company, I had my investment portion taken directly out of my check so that I never even saw it on payday. I had them send it into a totally separate account outside of my primary account. This way I was paying myself first every time I got paid. This removed the money from my hands. It allowed me to pay into my future every pay period. It removed the temptation to spend the money because I never even saw the money.

You can do this too. Get that money out of your hands quickly. Do not even let it touch your fingers. Our fingers get really sticky when it comes to money. We instantly come up with all kinds of ideas of what we can do with the money. If you pay yourself first by having it sent to a separate account, then it removes the temptation. After a while you will become comfortable with this and you won't even miss it. Try it. Try to get up to a minimum of 10% of everything that you make to pay to yourself, and do it first, not after everyone else. Before taxes, not after taxes. Reducing your taxes is an entire book in and of itself, but I am confident that you will read a book on that subject because you now understand the importance of education for your success.

Many wealthy people donate money also. As I stated before it is my belief to give a portion to the church also. I'll tell you this, by using the method just outlined in this chapter, my home does not go lacking in any regard. Pattern yourself after wealthy people. They realize the importance of sowing into their future and the future of their family. You are priceless, don't ever forget that. Stop putting the welfare of these companies before the well being of your own future.

CHAPTER 21

WHERE DO RICH PEOPLE INVEST?

So we have figured out our true financial position by doing a brief and very simplified net worth analysis. We now understand why rich people invest. We now understand when rich people invest. The last question is where do rich people invest?

Once again I stress to you that the approach that I recommend concerning most endeavors regarding obtaining success is to take advice from or follow a successful pattern of someone, or some group, that has already accomplished what we are trying to accomplish. If you have a successful career in whatever you choose to involve yourself in, inevitably there will follow an increase in salary compared to your present position. We must be wise in the handling of these finances if we are to have control over our future.

So where do rich people invest their money? Let's start by looking at where un-rich people invest their money. Once again the concept is quite simple. Rich people put their money into things that increase in value, and un-rich people tend to put their money into things that decrease in value.

Let's specifically look at where many blacks put their money. I can only speak from my experience, and I do not want to paint any-one with the same broad brush, but we must be honest with each other if we are to move forward. Let's look into some of our black homes in our major cities. Hold off for a second, let's not even go inside of the home. Let's just focus on the outside of the home for a moment. In the black neighborhoods how many times have we seen a very expensive car parked in the driveway of a run down home? All of us have seen this scenario played out over and over. If it makes no sense, then why is it such a common occurrence?

All too often some of us tend to put a very large proportion of our income into cars. We have to get out of the mindset of, "I can afford the car payment, so I can afford the car." It is not whether or not you can afford the payment. That is why they make the payment affordable, so you will buy the car. The question should be, is this large percentage of my income going into something that is going to increase in value or something that is going to decrease in value? For many of us, our car note combined with insurance payment is our second highest monthly expense behind our rent/mortgage pay-ment.

It is the second highest expense we have, and we dump these large sums of money into something that decreases in value. This is not how rich people think. Rich people put their money into things that increase in value and minimize the amounts of money that they dump into things that decrease in value.

Think of your favorite car. It doesn't matter if you can afford it yet or if you have acquired it already. Get that picture in your mind. No matter what type of car it is, the minute that you drive it off of the lot, it starts to decrease in value. I don't care if you go and get a Mercedes or a BMW or whatever it is. It will decrease in value as time goes on. Well, what kind of investment is that? Exactly, a bad one. It is not an investment, but it is an expense that constantly declines in value every year. It's no wonder that we fail to accumulate wealth when we constantly make our second highest expense something that is guaranteed to lose money every time.

Why do we continue to spend our money this way? Because no one has taught us any different. No one taught us how to keep our money. We have plenty of examples on how to spend our money. This is why education is so vital to our success.

I hear you now, "But I see wealthy people in expensive cars all of the time, what do you mean that this is not how they think?" Of course you see wealthy people in expensive cars, that's who they make that stuff for. Remember I said percentages of income. Wealthy people minimize the percentage of their funds that are placed into things that decrease in value. So yes, you will see wealthy people in expensive cars, but it is a very small percentage of their net worth equation. Many times, we make an automobile along with the insurance premiums a very large portion of our expenses. If the second largest contributor to your net worth equation is something that declines in value then how do you ever expect to accumulate wealth? You will not increase your net worth by accumulating something that constantly decreases in value. Let's have another look at the net worth equation.

ASSETS

$500   = Bank Accounts (checking, savings, money markets)

$0   = Stocks, Bonds, Mutual funds, other investments i.e. Real estate

$150,000 = Current Appraised value of home (primary residence)

$20,000   = Value of Auto

$0   = 401k or other investment vehicles

$170,500 = Total assets

LIABILITIES

$10,000 =All of your current bills, including credit cards

$140,000 = Mortgage owed

$27,000 =Automobile loans

$20,000 = Student loans (ouch)

$10,000 = Any other outstanding loans i.e. home equity loans

$207,000 = Total liabilities

ASSETS MINUS LIABILITIES = NET WORTH = (-$36,500)

       As you can see, the money that you have to pay for the car goes on the negative side of the equation, not the positive side of the equation. Everything that you bought last year on that credit card goes on the negative side of the equation.

       Don't get me wrong, I enjoy beautiful material items also. But what I am trying to get you to understand is that you are doing your future harm when you purchase these items that decrease in value with a very large percentage of your income. There is an order to doing things if you are to be successful. If you put priority on obtaining things before obtaining wealth, then the wealth will never come. Why? Because you will spend your whole life paying for all of these things instead of accumulating wealth.

The concept of where rich people invest is quite simple, they invest the majority of their funds in things that increase in value and minimize the amounts of funds that are placed into things that decrease in value. Rich people spend there finances building the asset column and less of their income goes into the liability column. If you have a strong enough asset column you will be able to purchase as many of the liabilities as you like.

I go into some peoples homes at times and have to run back to the front door and check to see what neighborhood I'm in. I have to make sure that I'm not in Beverly Hills somewhere. We have three or four televisions, one of them probably a wide screen. We have multiple VCR's and DVD players. We have very expensive stereos. We have so many pairs of shoes and clothes that we can't even wear them all. We have beautiful watches and on and on and on. You know what I am talking about. If you look in the closets, what you will see is all of the latest fashions. Every single one of these items decline in value, they do not increase. So as you can see, determining how well your financial situation is doing based on what you can afford or how much stuff you have is very flawed. It gives you a false sense of security.

You can have a house full of stuff and be one paycheck away from being on the street. Why? Because all of these items decrease in value, they do not increase. You need to increase your assets and decrease your liabilities. If you fall behind on your house payments, you cannot take your fancy shoes down to the mortgage company in an exchange for the amount that you owe them. They want money, period. This should show you that those expensive shoes hold no value to anyone except yourself. On a balance sheet, they are worth absolutely nothing. The next time you apply for a loan or a credit card pay close attention to the questions that they ask you. It will give you a better idea of what has value in the financial world. They never ask you if you have a big screen TV, do they? No, because it is worth nothing to them. They want to know the balance of bank accounts, how much property you own, how many assets you have in investments, etc. These are things that hold value. When you apply for a mortgage, they could care less about your designer jeans because they hold no value no matter how much you paid for them.

Once again let me stress that there is nothing wrong with material things. I enjoy them also. But if you are going to keep what you make, you must place more of your money into things that increase in value instead of a majority of your money into things that decrease in value. The next time you are about to purchase something that costs over $100, ask yourself if this is something that is going to increase in value or something that is going to decrease in value. I promise that it will change your spending habits. The minute that you educate yourself and start to change your spending habits will be the very minute that your ship will change course and becomes directed towards financial success.

CHAPTER 22

PROPER PERSPECTIVE

"For What Does It Profit A Man To Gain The Whole World And Lose His Soul"
-Jesus the Christ

We often hear people say, "Keep things in their proper per-spective." I believe that this is a very important statement. All too often we chase things with all of our might and when we finally achieve them, we find that it really wasn't worth chasing. Many times we see things and believe that the reason that we are not happy is because we are without certain titles, money, or material goods. We constantly tell ourselves that if we only had this or if we only had that, then we would be happy.

I do not want anyone reading this book to think that obtaining an education or making more money will solve every one of his or her problems, because that just is not true. Do not look to these things as the source of your happiness because I promise you that you will be greatly disappointed.

Let me share something with you that an old man once shared with me. He told me that there are a few things that you will never hear a man say on his death bed. A man on his death bed never says that he should have worked more hours. A man on his death bed never says, "Darn, I should have worked one more double shift." A man on his death bed never says that he should have made more money. When people are at the end of life, and realize that it really is about to be over, these are the types of things that they say. "I should have developed a stronger relationship with the Lord." "I should have spent more time with my children." "I should have been nicer to my wife." "I should have done more to help other people."

I did what the slogan says that every red-blooded American should do, go to school, get an education, and get a good job. I did that. There are very few jobs in America that get you more respect than when you tell someone that you are a surgeon. After I did it, I looked around as if to say, "Now what?" "Is this it?" It was not until I came into the knowledge of God and developed a personal relationship with him did I really know what true happiness was.

If you are not happy before you get your fancy car and your big house, obtaining those things will not bring you happiness. There will be excitement for a while but it will soon fade when the newness is gone. Education, success, and money are like the icing and the candles, not the substance of the cake itself. Keep things in their proper perspective.

Sincerely,
Roderick Claybrooks, M.D.

Give The Gift of The Black Student's Guide to Success
To Your Friends and Colleagues
www.blackstudentsguide.com

Check Your Local Bookstore or Order Here

Yes, I want _____ copies of The Black Student's Guide to Success
$15.95 each

Include $3.95 shipping and handling for one book, and $1.95 for each additional book. Michigan residents add $0.96 sales tax per book.

Payment must accompany orders. Allow 3 weeks for delivery.

My check or money order for $_____ is enclosed.

Name:_____

Organization:_____

Address:_____

City/State/Zip:_____
P h o n e : _
Email_____

Call (313) 204-5572 for questions

Make your check payable and return to
Plasmid Publishing House
P.O. Box 39201
Redford, MI. 48239
Fax (313) 387-9879

Order online at www.blackstudentsguide.com